EVERY SILVER LINING
HAS A CLOUD

EVERY SILVER LINING HAS A CLOUD

Relapse and the Symptoms of Sobriety

Scott Stevens

Copyright © 2012 by Scott Stevens.

Library of Congress Control Number:		2012922710
ISBN:	Hardcover	978-1-4797-5949-1
	Softcover	978-1-4797-5948-4
	Ebook	978-1-4797-5950-7

All rights reserved. No part of this book may be reproduced or transmitted in any form or by any means, electronic or mechanical, including photocopying, recording, or by any information storage and retrieval system, without permission in writing from the copyright owner.

Also by Scott Stevens:
"What the Early Worm Gets"

Visit alcohologist.com or email whattheearlywormgets@gmail.com for more information. Twitter @AlcoholAuthor.

This book was printed in the United States of America.

To order additional copies of this book, contact:
Xlibris Corporation
1-888-795-4274
www.Xlibris.com
Orders@Xlibris.com
124614

Acknowledgements

Norma, KS, LKS, JW and Xlibris all have been valuable sounding boards for my ramblings and have helped focus the message. For that, I'm very grateful. The dozens of people I personally interviewed are owed plenty of thanks for sharing their experiences. I have credited nearly 80 sources throughout this work: All professionals I admire and respect. Their leadership in the field of alcohology is an inspiration.

Sherry at Agape, Valley Hope Chandler and Tempe, Sheriff Jeff, Steve at Pinnacle Legal Services, the 12 & 12 Club and Bloopers Club: Thank all of you for your wisdom and integrity.

I appreciate the help and support of everyone who's been along with me over the two years that went into this book, especially my mother and sister, the mother of my children and, of course, the two most brilliant children in the world. You are loved. Thank you for believing even when I didn't give you much in which to believe.

... The deeper the need that has been fulfilled, the deeper the gratitude.

Introduction

Sometimes the clichés get it right. Every cloud has a silver lining. Sobriety was the silver lining to a really calamitous dark cloud drinking was for me as it is for a lot of people. But it isn't all rainbows and unicorns once you're sober.

Just like *What the Early Worm Gets*, this book contains information I wish I had been given when I first detoxed or when I first lapsed or even when I first questioned my drinking. Some of it I might not have wanted to hear. Some of it *you* might not want to hear. Alcoholism doesn't come in tidy, easy-to-manage packages though. It isn't simple and sobriety isn't consequence-free like other popular silver linings today promising tighter abs, better sex, dramatic weight loss, a blissful life or whiter teeth: People can and do die if they don't get sobriety right.

There is something for most in these pages. If you drink, have stopped, know someone who has, or even if you've never had a drop, there's something for you in here. Not because my writing is that peerless but because the facts I present (my own and others) are solid, urgent and universal. Alcohol is so large a part of our health as individuals and as a country: Sobriety's stakes are that high.

If you are not Alcoholic and have sat back and watched in horror as a sober Alcoholic slipped back into drinking and wondered what the hell would make him go back to the misery, this book is as much for you as it is for the Alcoholic.

Every Silver Lining Has a Cloud isn't a crusade to cure people. I'm inept at both crusades and cures. I'm no evangelist, either. I'm a reporter. I only inform to make sure people know alcohol's story, to reveal what's behind relapse, to illustrate a path to get the right help to the right people. I've included views of psychiatrists, psychologists, geneticists, sociologists, biochemists and medical doctors. And Alcoholics. And their families. I've largely left out the views of the beverage industry, legislators, trade groups (notably the National Council of State Legislators) and special interests (notably MADD) because of their respective agendas. In that regard, I haven't lived up to my journalistic training in covering both sides of the story or maintaining objectivity throughout. But it is independent: I'm not looking for clients, donors or converts.

This is personal. Intensely personal.

I put some of my darkest times into this book, the darkest days of my sobriety. My successes are here, too, but mostly some vivid, ugly, painful failures. Success is more fun, but failure is a better teacher. In the previous book, I bemoaned my fear of how incarceration threatened to undo all the positive my family and I gained from the voluntary rehab I made a priority. I had facts that bore out the legitimacy of that fear and then I became a statistic proving it true. It was no self-fulfilling prophesy. It surely wasn't intentional. It was, however, a good teacher. That's the lesson of the next 11 chapters.

Not all useful knowledge, after all, comes from laboratory experiments or theory. I know how phony it sounds when someone who has lived a life unchallenged by alcohol preaches about alcohol or Alcoholism and especially lapse or relapse. When you see charts on Page 125 or APPENDIX I, for example, it's one thing to read them as verifiable, clinical fact, but they have meaning when the source giving you the charts is someone who's actually lived on those peaks and valleys, someone who's felt the symptoms, someone who's experienced recovery and relapse and has hit a bottom. Or two.

My personal insights are combined with those of more than 280 relapsers and findings published in more than 70 sources. I'm confident I've gotten more right than wrong and that's validated by the works of hundreds before me. I don't presume to replace any of the body of work on Alcoholism already published, only to add to it. It's not important who's more right. It's important that we're having a dialogue about the pain Alcoholism can still carry *after getting sober.*

If you hear yourself in here, it's not too late. If you hear someone you care about, ask them about it and begin the conversation. Get them to hear their voices not mine.

Every Silver Lining Has a Cloud

==The pain an Alcoholic feels is the pain of self-loathing and humiliation ... from loss of respect== ... from isolation and loneliness ... from awareness that he is throwing away much of his uniqueness ... from gradually destroying his body and soul. That pain doesn't just vanish when you walk away from the bottle. The silver lining has a cloud.

Sobriety has its stressors which are confounded by a biochemical flaw recently discovered in Alcoholics. Relieving the stress with alcohol is fun or at least consequence free for a non-Alcoholic. It's a chore for an Alcoholic who faces a return to a nightmare of retching, vertigo, shakes and razor-edged regret. Nobody would consciously choose that, especially after legal or family troubles, the likes of which I chronicled in the previous book. Yet thousands relapse every day. It's the baffling nature of the disease.

Wondering why an Alcoholic goes back to alcohol after finally getting sober is like wondering why when we give a little boy two die-cast cars the first thing he does is SMASH them into each other. "It just happens that way." Right? "It's how we're wired." Isn't it? I needed better answers because I did go back to alcohol.

Chapter One

"I was cured all right."
—the last words of Alex in the U.S. version of
A Clockwork Orange, Anthony Burgess, 1962

October 17, 2010. Two days after *What the Early Worm Gets* was on press, I lapsed. That's three and a half years into my recovery following voluntary treatment . . . and *during* a state-run alcohol program I was forced to attend.

I didn't wake up on the 17th saying, "I'm drinking today," or "The Packers are on TV, I think I'll have a couple." I didn't intend to blow the recovery I had going. Just that morning while struggling with my concentration and recently poor sleep, I read from *Alcoholics Anonymous*, (a.k.a. The Big Book) to try to get a little perspective or maybe some of their famous serenity. God knows I had none of either. I recall reading the following from Chapter 2, "There is a Solution," a chapter I found helpful if not encouraging.

> "The fact is that most alcoholics . . . have lost the power of choice in drink. Our so-called will-power becomes practically non-existent. We are unable at certain times to bring into our consciousness with sufficient force the memory of the suffering and humiliation of even a week or a month ago. We are without defense against the first drink. The almost certain consequences that follow taking even a glass of beer do not crowd into the mind to deter us . . . There is a complete failure of the kind of defense that keeps one from putting his hand on a hot stove." (*Alcoholics Anonymous*, AA World Services, 1939)

My sobriety so far was no defense because I was suffering from it, in what are identified later as Symptoms of Sobriety. Despite the time invested in getting and staying sober, I was struggling with it. Couldn't concentrate. Couldn't seem to remember squat. Irritable. And more than a little resentful that I felt so low and this was supposed to be the silver lining.

Everything is easy until it gets complicated.

I was struggling with a new burst of confidence and self-worth, too, because I should have been happy with early book orders and from speaking engagements I was beginning to put on the calendar. Instead I felt guilt? "What business did I have regaining confidence?" is how I questioned my worthiness of the happiness and confidence and comfort. I'd had that kind of sick thinking shamed into me the preceding weeks while I was attending the mandated substance abuse program not designed for Alcoholism. So instead of a rewarding feeling earned and deserved, I was uncomfortable with the confidence the criminal justice system told me I no longer deserved. It's a message I internalized.

I was still feeling ill, or uncomfortable, or *dis*eased after reading the 12-step stuff. That was enough of a warning sign for me to call someone in my support network to try to keep the conflict, shame and guilt from turning into a lapse. I even text messaged the counselor from the program. (Even though it was a Sunday, he made it clear there wasn't a boundary issue about contacting him when my sobriety was at stake.)

I had no call returned, no text answered. Anytime.

As the morning progressed, the inability to concentrate and the edginess grew more desperate. I made it through the football game without the returned calls. My team lost to Miami in overtime but that wasn't an ingredient in the drinking that was about to come down: I'm a huge fan but drinking to the wins and drinking away the losses was never part of my repertoire.

I had to move—change scenery and mind. The local apple orchard was open. I went there a few days earlier and decided to go back there today to seek that change. That place has been special to me since I was a kid in my mostly rural Wisconsin county. We went there as a family to get apples and feed the goats the cores of the apples I sampled. Fond, dear memories. Nothing like nostalgia and positive memories combined with fresh air to get my head in the right place. This part of small-town, no-deadbolts-or-gang-bangers, not-country-but-not-suburban Wisconsin still spoke to my soul despite having lived in the nation's largest metros and having walked the country's corridors of power. The orchard usually grounded me and righted me. It was "home" to me and the orchard, the fall air, even the damn goats had to throw me a rope out of the confusion and frustration I was feeling.

But I didn't go straight there. I went for a walk first.

Right past the convenience store . . .

That sells liquor.

I bought two bottles of 86-proof and drained most of both.
It was pure impulse.

It's like an old girlfriend who winks at you or drops you an email out of the blue. You KNOW better. You know to hit delete or keep walking. I wish I hadn't lost that lesson because once I took that first gulp, just like anyone with Alcoholism, *not* taking the second gulp is like trying to slam a revolving door.

In 2000 and again in 2004 I cried tears of happiness, the greatest happiness, when my children were born. October 17, 2010, as the alcohol seared its way down to my stomach, I cried different tears, tears loaded with as much emotion, only it was sadness because my lapse was here and I was disappointing those two amazing children. Again.

I went from discomfort at dawn, to confusion at 3:00 p.m. Then to the hospital and a .384 blood alcohol concentration (BAC, .08 is considered illegal intoxication for motorists, .30 and higher is usually associated with coma or death). This BAC was not close to the ridiculous levels of my previous drinking career. This is a remarkable demonstration of the progressive nature of the disease even while it's in remission. After lengthy abstinence I was immediately able to ratchet up my BAC to lethal levels without a sign of slurring or trouble walking. So I got behind the wheel. My motor skills may have been ok, but the judgment was clearly screwed. I still wanted to hit the orchard and, another great idea, drive over to a friend's house with the hope that she'd intervene with my drinking. Great thinking.

I was arrested. There was no collision, but that's beside the point. I was a menace just by being on the road in that condition and posing a danger to everyone. There are no bad OWI arrests. I regret the poor judgment. And I really regret losing my sobriety.

How could this happen after going through treatment and while I was in mistreatment? After changing the people, places and things associated with my most severe drinking days, just as prescribed by nearly every reputable counselor, I'm drinking? After all those 12-step meetings? After fixing my diet and exercise? Hell, I even took Pilates for a bit to fix the whole "mind/body" thing, and I'm drinking? I was well past being an acute and toxic Alcoholic, far beyond cravings, and well into sobriety. And I hit .384, just like that.

I needed to return to treatment. To get the lapse put away before it turned to relapse and to get those answers. And maybe sort out the confusion and confidence issues while I was there. Treatment was not where I was going, though, despite wanting to be there and by all indications needing to be there. I was heading back to jail instead. To "learn." You know because they taught me so well the last time.

The list of 13 things in my last book I "learned" by being incarcerated had nothing to do with recovery and everything to do with being a slick criminal with some really warped aberrant behavior. To that list, I can now add these lessons from the rehabilitation environment:

14. That you Armor All your gun so fingerprints cannot be left on a weapon.
15. The price of fishing lures being what they are today, you can resell "lost" fishing lures hung up on underwater snags *you* create. Anglers gladly repurchase them, so long as you don't let on that you sank a mattress box spring in hot spots to snare their lures.
16. That I, too, can be a pimp. (That's coming up in Chapter Ten)
17. I learned how to make meth in a soda bottle and order hybrid marijuana seeds on the internet for home growing.

More skills of questionable value for keeping me clear of whiskey.

Incarceration again failed to provide sobriety tools. I was wrong, again for drinking and driving and should have been behind bars for breaking the law. But this wasn't help for the underlying problem. I was again left to produce the lessons myself against a backdrop of some pretty severe degenerates who wanted nothing to do with their kids and families, real jobs, real sobriety or the real society to which most people not locked up want to contribute rather than mock. In *The Early Worm*, I mentioned that incarceration isn't hard for the hardest criminals, but it is tremendously hard punishment and traumatic for people who've achieved something with their lives and never lived for the criminal code or the thrill of misdeeds. It's not just dangerous and debasing. It's a daily strain against insanity, a constant struggle to resist becoming numb and institutionalized. And it's abusive. Mothers fret over the wellbeing of their kids no matter what age. Death of the child would probably be more comforting than the prolonged abuse of being locked up. I'd have spared my mom this grief had I simply drank myself to death October 17, 2010. Little did I know that I nearly had: The BAC was the same as what killed singer Amy Winehouse.

But I *didn't* die and learned more about the cloud behind the silver lining of sobriety, learning what really leads to lapse years after stopping drinking, what are the symptoms and why nearly every Alcoholic relapses.

Chapter Two

"If at first you don't succeed, you're running about average."
—M.H. Alderson

I'm going to flex a little research muscle in this chapter, but it's worth wading through one chapter of some bigger words and nerdy studies here to get to some of the feeling in the chapters beyond because some newer science is very revealing.

My relapse had as much to do with a gland taking up a cubic inch atop each kidney as it did with the disease of Alcoholism itself and little to do with the convenience store or the Pilates or the people/places/things I changed in my sobriety or renegade thoughts of being able to drink like "normal" people. The glands are the adrenal glands. New research supports the conclusion that the disease *and relapse* are biochemical and especially that relapse is not a deliberate, willful decision. As reported in *Alcoholism: Clinical and Experimental Research* in October 2010, the culprit behind lapse or relapse is one of the substances produced and secreted by the adrenals. Cortisol is the biochemical to which the research points, confirming that just as there is a biochemical source to Alcoholism, there is a biochemical flaw that can trip up our best efforts to stay sober.

Specifically the researchers found that cortisol—an adrenal product secreted in response to stressors—is found in high levels in Alcoholics, even those in recovery, even those with long periods of abstinence. The cortisol contributes to the high rate of lapse/relapse. In non-Alcoholics, only traces of cortisol are released and only in times of high emotional reaction or prolonged stress. In Alcoholics, the study found constant levels instead, and levels that were consistently higher than those found in a non-Alcoholic undergoing an excessively stressful episode. The 2010 study follows a 2003 study published in the same journal and conducted by the University of Texas Southwestern Medical Center at Dallas, which first showed an alcohol/cortisol link and demonstrated that all drinkers, Alcoholics or Alcohol Abusers (see APPENDIX II for the difference) experience two to three times higher salivary cortisol levels from drinking when compared to abstinent individuals. Furthermore, cortisol concentrations increased during the progression from intoxication to withdrawal. The 2010 study indicates the change is permanent.

The Alcoholic's cortisol baseline is higher than the non-Alcoholic's for one of three reasons: We're born that way (genetics); or damage caused by acetaldehyde (a by-product of the metabolism of alcohol) to the glands that produce cortisol; or acetaldehyde damage to the brain structure—the pituitary—which regulates cortisol levels. A fourth theory for the higher baseline cortisol is that the glands producing the cortisol are overused from being under prolonged exposure to stress.

Cortisol, epinephrine and norepinephrine are the chemicals produced by the adrenal glands. Epinephrine and norepinephrine are also known as adrenaline and noradrenaline and are secreted at much higher levels than the lesser known stress hormone cortisol. Cortisol is also known as hydrocortisone when manufactured synthetically or sold over-the-counter as a first aid ointment commonly applied to skin irritations. Hydrocortisone, used that way, is soothing. Cortisol in the bloodstream isn't.

People would not survive without these adrenal gland chemicals. The stress hormones give us ability to react and respond to threats. The brain monitors the conditions in and around its owner and orchestrates it owner's behavior through the biochemical signals to optimize the owner's chances of survival, e.g. eat, don't get eaten, reproduce. That's how primitive the level of our biochemistry is.

Ages ago it served an important role as part of the fight-or-flight response (also connected to adrenaline and noradrenaline) which helped keep our ancestors alive. Fight-or-flight is adrenal glands' ancient biochemical reaction to stress of survival. First, norepinephrine triggered the release of sugars into the bloodstream so you could sustain battle. Over the longer battle, cortisol is released by the outer section of the gland—a structure called the adrenal cortex—to press more sugars into the bloodstream for your fight or your flight. The excess sugars can contribute to diabetes . . . more on that in just a moment . . . but they also become acids when not expended as fuel for muscles running away from charging woolly mammoths. The acids in the blood literally fry your brain, the organ you most need to overcome sobriety's symptoms.

When your brain is fried, the acids inhibit information processing. You're prone to making poor emotional, financial and life decisions. Ironic that the biochemicals that helped propel us away from peril millennia ago, today bring us toward emotional or financial peril. Seems running away from frightening beasts would have been the better battle.

Cortisol creates acid, acid fries the brain, the brain causes confusion. It slows you, frustrates you, especially when your fried brain makes mistakes. And it will.

In this millennium when an Alcoholic or non-Alcoholic who is brand new at something—like public speaking or ice skating or sobriety—you experience surges of adrenaline and cortisol in smaller amounts because the brain senses its owner may have a survival threat. Once a human masters the skill like public speaking or skating, you still get a small "adrenaline" rush, but a healthy adrenal cortex functioning properly wouldn't release cortisol because you've mastered the skill. There is no longer a threat to survival. (In today's reality there never was one: You weren't getting eaten, after all.) When cortisol is still produced in swells by poorly functioning adrenal cortex, it affects almost all body functions, creating discomfort. That fried feeling.

Neuroendocrinologist Dr. Bruce McEwen in a 1999 Science of Cognition Conference in Washington, D.C. revealed groundbreaking research connecting cortisol to brain cell damage and even memory failure and behavioral changes. McEwen demonstrated that cortisol has a direct influence on a cell's nucleus and also regulates liver metabolism. This is already an organ and a function that are genetically compromised. (See *What the Early Worm Gets* for a discussion of alcohol dehydrogenase, a liver enzyme controlled by the chromosome defects behind the disease of Alcoholism.) So, while we needed cortisol once upon a time for survival, it compromises the comfort of our survival when overproduced.

The 21st century human hasn't the same need for the fight-or-flight reflex upon which our ancestors relied. We are in no immediate danger of physical harm. That day of my relapse, I wasn't freezing in some cave or threatened by a charging beast. I had a value menu nearby, not a kill-or-be-killed hunt. Those neighboring tribes may be jacking up my property taxes, yet they weren't slinging flint-tipped arrows at my offspring or running a spear through me. My muscles had no need for fuel for a life-or-death battle. But I was swimming in cortisol because the Alcoholic body produces too much of it when little or none at all was needed. Our stressors are of a lower grade these days, but for those of us with Alcoholism, even the lowest stressors put more cortisol in the system that already has a higher level of it to begin with. For the Alcoholic in recovery, the increased cortisol secretion is problematic and has been documented in several stress, depression, sleep or health studies conducted between the two mentioned above.

The cortisol response, however, is a reflex and not one you can shut off. Some reflexes, called orienting reflexes, can fade rapidly upon repetition, a process called habituation. An example is the response from tapping the tendon below your kneecap, which causes the quadriceps to contract and the leg to extend. You can't shut the reflex off, but it diminishes if you keep tapping. Not so with the cortisol response to stress, called an adaptive reflex, which cannot be habituated. An example is how the eye's pupil contracts in bright light. The encouraging thing is that the adaptive reflex of the cortisol *can* be controlled by reducing the Symptoms of Sobriety just like the pupil's contraction is controlled by the brightness of the light.

Physical signs of too much cortisol include easier bruising, acne, increased blood pressure and swollen ankles. Dr. Paul Donohue, who writes "To Your Health," a syndicated newspaper column adds, "It increases sugar production within the body and can lead to diabetes," also approaching epidemic status globally, though in most cases not connected to cortisol but to diet. "It [cortisol] breaks down protein, and thereby weakens muscles. It redistributes fat. Fat leaves the arms and legs and deposits in the face and trunk. It makes a person more susceptible to infection. It can bring about cataracts. It can also lead to osteoporosis."

Too much cortisol also creates an exaggerated startle response, confusion and mood changes like irritability. These non-physiological reactions to cortisol have a direct connection to lapse/relapse and are to what I'm referring when I use the term Symptoms of Sobriety.

Ironically, research from the University of Chicago showed conclusively what does block cortisol. Alcohol. "Alcohol can decrease the cortisol the body releases to respond to stress," says Emma Childs, a research associate at the university quoted in *Alcoholism: Clinical and Experimental Research*, October 2011. That's one of the many paradoxes of alcohol and the Alcoholic: The quick, easy solution to cortisol giving you the Symptoms is to *drink*. After all, relieving stress is the number one or two reason most people, including non-Alcoholics, drink. Lapse or relapse is, obviously, a ridiculous alternative that only makes the stress—and the cortisol—worse in the long term. In the hand of an Alcoholic alcohol is no answer, it is a question: "What do you feel like losing today?"

Before I continue with the Symptoms of Sobriety, first I'd like to clarify: Lapse and relapse are not interchangeable terms in this book, a view disputed by some alcohologists but shared by the likes of Dr. Mark Willenbring, Director of the National Institute on Alcohol Abuse and Alcoholism. The treatment pros at Hazelden call a lapse "being close without using" and relapse "using," and they undisputedly have more books than I do. But for this book, lapse is an episode. Like me on October 17, 2010. Alcoholics Anonymous calls it a slip. You fall off the wagon and have a drink or several. Relapse is several episodes. You return to an Alcoholic drinking pattern.

Both are considered by alcohologists to be part of the recovery process, yet some cynically state that relapse isn't part of recovery it's part of drinking. Terence Gorski, author of *Staying Sober*, (Herald House/Independence Press, Independence, MO 1986) is the pioneer of the Relapse Prevention Protocol and he believes "you cannot experience recovery without experiencing a tendency toward relapse." Louise Bailey Burgess, author of *Alcohol and Your Health*, (Charles Publishing, Los Angeles 1973) adds, "Unfortunately, despite desperate determination, the depressing fact remains that not more than 50 percent of those who decide to quit, manage to attain sobriety for the rest of their lives." Neuroscientist George Koob of the Scripps Research Institute, in *Close to Home: Moyers on Addiction*, (Public Affairs Television, Hamilton, NJ 1998) puts the number at 80 percent of those who have detoxed relapsing within a year. Yet another expert, Michael Dennis of Chestnut Health Systems says in, *Addiction: Why Can't They Just Quit?* (HBO Home Video, New York 2007). "Seventy percent of patients relapse after the first time getting help. It's not like fixing a broken bone."

The high rate of lapse (or relapse) isn't even unique to Alcoholics. People with chronic depression have a relapse rate also at 50-80 percent. High blood pressure patients only have to keep taking their meds—a really simple task compared to staying clear of alcohol—and their rate of non-compliance is as high. Patients with seizure disorders: Same thing. Diabetics? Ditto . . . high rate of relapse/non-compliance. Asthmatics are even worse. Relapse *is* a part of having a chronic disease. "Bill," a man I've come to appreciate and respect over the years relapsed *four times in 20 months*.

A lapse or relapse doesn't mean the end of your recovery. Your life doesn't return to the previous chaos just from one lapse or relapse. Recovery is stability, stable psychosocial status to which you *can return* even after a lapse if you promptly correct it and not let it turn to loss of control. You don't go all the way back to the start just from a lapse once you begin recovery. That's the fatalistic thinking that dooms a thousand recoveries a day. Dr. Alan Marlatt in *Relapse Prevention*, (Guilford Publishing, New York 1985) refers to that flawed thinking as self-fulfilling prophesy because if you earnestly believe you are doomed if you lapse, you WILL lapse. And be wary of those who would suggest that you tell yourself that "lapse and relapse are part of recovery" just to make yourself feel better about a slip. Nobody "feels better" about a relapse and no one is going to be harder on you than yourself about a lapse, regardless of building such a sophisticated justification beforehand. What's important is not how hard you are on yourself or how you "justify" anything, it's what you do to get back to sobriety rather than keeping drinking. "Bill," for example, lapsed four times but tried fighting off the Symptoms of Sobriety *five times*. His full name: Bill Wilson, the founder of AA. The experts know that it can and often does take lapse or relapse—often more than one—for someone to stay sober. That's the good news. After two or three lapses and another kick at the cat, over half MAKE IT to permanent sobriety, according to Dennis. They reach a state of sustained recovery.

Lapse comes from stressors. Recovery creates stress. Stress exaggerates your cortisol problem. Your fried brain, bombarded with acids and cortisol is triggered into a neurochemical war between serotonin and dopamine (see *What the Early Worm Gets* for a discussion on the Big Two neurochemicals and their imbalance being a genetic flaw in Alcoholics). You can't Pilates your way out from all the stressors sobriety pimps out of your day-to-day life.

In several regards, the difficulties of Attention Deficit Hyperactivity Disorder (ADHD) are shockingly similar to the faulty output experienced when your brain is stormed with cortisol and acids. Dr. McEwen concluded that like ADHD sufferers, those in the grip of cortisol overload cannot filter out random data that's unproductive, so your brain acts on *all* inputs. "All inputs" includes the message from an Alcoholic's diseased tissues that they need alcohol. That message conflicts with your sobriety messages and your mind's desire to stay sober. That's two inputs, two impulses, that overload each other and overwhelm you—an overload similar to ADHD that creates the Symptoms of Sobriety.

Stress, Cortisol and Symptoms of Sobriety

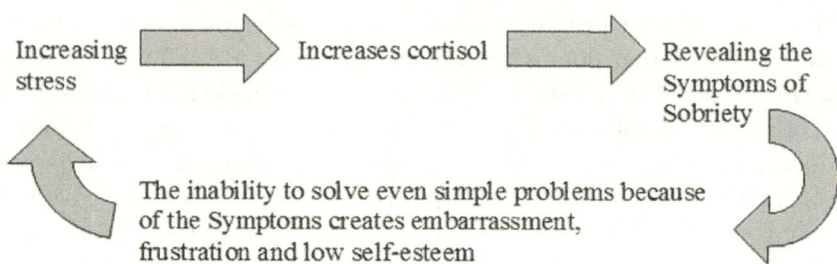

Cortisol is not the driver of relapse. Cortisol is the result of stress that drives the Symptoms of Sobriety. "You need to cite the driver, not the automobile," as Woodrow Wilson said. My effort to manage my Symptoms of Sobriety left out the stressors which drove the Symptoms. I didn't know the connection. I was treating the Symptom, not the cause. It's a peculiar way of thinking but not solely reserved for Alcoholics: How many times do people take acetaminophen for a headache, but resume the activity that gives them the headache?

Cortisol didn't buy those bottles . . . I'm responsible for that and for not being attentive to *why* I was feeling lousy to begin with. I didn't realize stressors were the cause of the Symptoms of Sobriety. It wasn't in my training to look for the causes. I've found I'm not alone in that because in most training (a.k.a. rehab) People, Places and Things are commonly viewed as the triggers for a lapse, so you're programmed to work out of your life the bad PP&T. If you hang with a drinking crowd, you'll drink again, so the programming goes. You have places that trigger you, like dining at a certain eatery, same result. These things are true. Very true. But WHY do you go hang around those people? WHY do you go to those places? Because they're no-stress situations. Seeking comfort and familiarity are entirely human reactions when we feel uncomfortable. The programming just tells you to knock it off . . . not to look for what the stressor is.

The Symptoms need to be understood from the perspective that while sobriety may seem to be the objective—the silver lining—for Alcoholics, sobriety is actually a state of *dis*ease. *Dis*ease means your body has lost balance. Think of it like being dehydrated. You're not back in balance just by drinking another glass of water, you're still ill until your body's tissues signal they're not. As an Alcoholic, once you begin treating the disease, you're still at *dis*ease because your tissues are still saying they need alcohol and your cortisol still signals that you're in peril. Sobriety then is only a step in a progression from disease to *dis*ease to recovery.

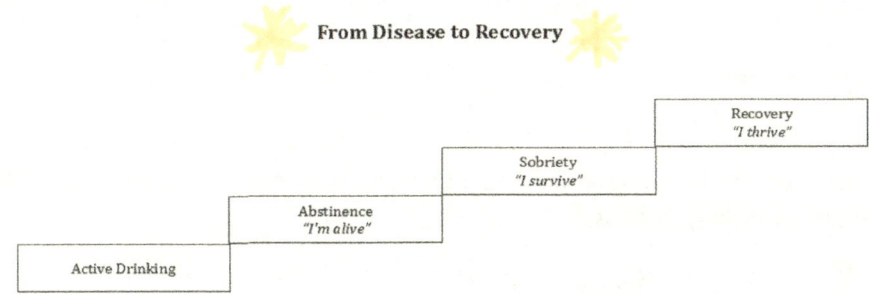

Abstinence is complying with keeping a toxic substance out of your tissues. You take away the alcohol and you are abstinent, not sober. You're not drinking but are still shaking like a colt on new legs. You think about the booze. You crave. That's not sobriety yet. You try to integrate not drinking into life. Recovery is the full adjustment and balance of you mind and your tissues to no longer using alcohol. Recovery has to do with how you're living, not how you're not drinking. Recovery is where you freely see that sobriety is a better thing to have than to lack. Sobriety is the state in between.

Time helps . . . a lot of the movement from sobriety to recovery has to do with the passage of time (though many put too much emphasis on putting a number on it, like X-months or years). Sobriety is learning how things feel again and how routine it becomes to not consume. It's the state of feeling *dis*eased but improving. You're wood that's been drying awhile but not quite ready for the fireplace. When you drink, you give a lot of energy to alcohol and in sobriety you begin to take it back and reinvest it wisely.

Many people use the words sobriety and recovery much the same as tire and wheel are mistakenly interchanged. You ask someone what a cars rolls on, the common response is four wheels. The car rolls on tires. The tires are secured on wheels. They don't mean the same thing. Sobriety is like the wheel, recovery; like the tire . . . where the rubber meets the road, so to speak.

Don't look at each step as a single step, but multiple steps. The Washington Monument is a single place, just like sobriety is a single place, but the monument has 898 steps. Recovery is a sealed envelope some people never get to open unfortunately because they get stopped on the steps along the way by the Symptoms of Sobriety.

The Symptoms of Sobriety are signs of imbalance in the body and symptoms that warn sobriety is in jeopardy. The Symptoms of Sobriety would be the Symptoms of Relapse if you don't take responsibility for them and address them in order to stay in sobriety.

There is no finish line.

Everyone knows what excess adrenaline feels like from roller coaster rides or being chased by the neighbor's dog. Here's what excess cortisol feels like. The Symptoms of Sobriety are:

1. Neglecting sleep/rest/eating
2. Poor memory recall
3. Confusion and lack of clear thinking e.g. you feel dazed or can't concentrate
4. Emotional sensitivity, e.g. you're irritable, defensive or weepy
5. Substitution cravings/habits (overdoing it at work or indulging in candy or tobacco are most reported
6. Isolation
7. Hyperalert and/or easily startled

Medicine works best on a simple equation:
More Symptoms = More Treatment; or
Fewer Symptoms = Less Treatment.
But if you don't even recognize these as Symptoms that Alcoholism is coming out of remission, you risk lapse because if they are not handled as Symptoms, too often, as with most every other disease in medicine, the equation is:
No Symptoms = NO TREATMENT.

Once you know to look for these, reading a looming Alcoholic lapse is as easy as reading alphabet blocks.

They come in any combination. They can be witnessed with the physiological reactions to cortisol overload, such as the bruising or blood pressure problems, or can be independent of any physical manifestation of cortisol. A blood or saliva test can confirm levels above the normal range, but you'll know from these symptoms.

If you notice a few of the seven Symptoms and they don't interfere with your ability to socialize or work or mind family responsibilities, you're situation is mild as far as lapse likelihood. If you have Symptoms and they clash with work or family life but you still keep up most of the time, consider it moderate. If you've missed work or blown off family responsibilities intentionally or unintentionally because of the Symptoms, your sobriety is in jeopardy.

One of the differences between this disease and most other chronic ones that is so difficult to communicate is that with Alcoholism, when you are the sickest and most acute, you don't feel sick because you're getting alcohol. When you arrest the disease by treating it, *that's* when you feel sick. In remission. First from withdrawal symptoms, naturally, but more so from cortisol and the Symptoms of Sobriety. With cancer, for example, you don't feel sickest when you've stopped the spread and gotten that disease into remission. You feel sickest when the cancer is most acute. Lyme disease or even the flu is the same way. An Alcoholic can feel the sick from the Symptoms well into remission, even eight to ten years after stopping the drinking, according to 1985 research from Clinton DeSoto, William O'Donnell, Linda Alfred and Charles Lopes ("Symptomology in Alcoholics at Various Stages of Abstinence" in *Alcoholism: Clinical and Experimental Research*, vol. 9 1985). That seems crazy: Other diseases don't behave this way in remission.

And you are *not* crazy. You just need some adjustments.

A diabetic, by comparison, would address the condition, not just symptoms, with small lifestyle adjustments. A *severe* diabetic would require more extensive life changes as well as professional help. He'd have an expert evaluate the meaning of his diabetic symptoms, wouldn't he? Here's another medical comparison. If migraine sufferers had the luxury of such clear warning signs as the Symptoms of Sobriety *before* the onset of a migraine, they'd take heed. Why should the Symptoms of Sobriety be evaluated any less thoroughly than the symptoms of diabetes or heeded less than the warning signs preceding a migraine? Neither diabetes nor migraines are as lethal as snapping Alcoholism out of remission.

The Symptoms aren't some tabloid fad or syndrome-of-the-week; they are real. You feel like crap. It's not imaginary. Not everyone will suffer from them though. For me, the third Symptom—the clarity—was my most pronounced and created the most havoc. I was so accustomed to thinking quickly on my feet. I believed the sharpness of the training as a journalist never dulled. At times though, even well after I stopped my two-liters-a-day drinking ordeal, I could not focus for more than 20 minutes at a time, couldn't remember things I didn't write down and had to re-read stuff to get the point. The cortisol was doing what the alcohol couldn't: Singeing my brain, messing with my sharpness and my mental function. (Of course drinking that much blunted my judgment but at least I could make bad decisions more quickly.) I know this as a Symptom *now*. And now the Symptom is my own primary warning sign that there *is* something wrong and I need to address it and fix one or more of the *sources* listed at the end of the chapter, not just the Symptom itself.

The Symptoms of Sobriety, not surprisingly, resemble the symptoms of Post-Traumatic Stress Disorder (PTSD). When you read that, however, I want to make it abundantly clear that an Alcoholic is not a victim like PTSD sufferers are. Only the symptoms and the cortisol are the same. The Symptoms, just like the reactions to PTSD, can be regenerative—which means they get better over time—degenerative—meaning they get worse over time, but are usually degenerative. There's a growing body of evidence that an Alcoholic diagnosis when coupled with some of the professional, personal and social losses sustained from Alcoholic use is, in fact, a trauma.

In the graph in APPENDIX I, your disease progresses well beyond what an Alcohol Abuser experiences, thus the "trauma" comparison. The Symptoms emerge on the upward slope on the right half of the graph out of the physical and personal devastation you caused on the left half. Each of the steps up the right half carries an emotional investment and potentially can be a stressor. The stressors stimulate the adrenal cortex to release cortisol. The cortisol then has an impact after prolonged exposure to the stressor on the right side of the graph. It's key to remember the right side has ups and downs. It's never victory after victory or constant advancement just because you stop drinking. The downs are the stress. You're walking up a hill with a yo-yo. Become distracted by the yo-yo's ups and downs and you're not looking at the fact your making progress up the hill. If you get distracted by the stress, you risk not finishing the climb up the right side of the chart. Once you're distracted by the stressors your bathing in the cortisol and the Symptoms emerge.

Increased stress from the downs on that side of the chart and the corresponding cortisol lead to a state of "free-floating anxiety" as Gorski defines it. A feeling of compulsion. "The person feels compelled to do something, anything, to relieve the anxiety, often adopting behaviors that temporarily relieve the stress." What's that mean to Alcoholics and non-Alcoholics alike? Drinking. The inevitable loss of control. At this stage it is essential to reactivate your recovery by addressing the underlying stressor, not just seek temporary relief from the Symptom. If you instead resort to treating only the Symptoms predictably an Alcoholic returns to alcohol.

As stressors increase, the Symptoms worsen. You have difficulty thinking clearly, managing emotions and remembering things. Here's the wild part of this condition: You are not on your A-game and thinking your clearest so you probably don't even consciously recognize the seven Symptoms as warning signs. Cortisol blocks your ability to assess yourself. Living without the ability to assess yourself is like being roommates with a Bengal tiger. You never know when it will take a lethal swipe at you, which in the case of the Alcoholic means seeking that temporary relief from a bottle.

The Symptoms *are* cumulative and can creep up on you. It's never, "WHAM, here I am." One will pop up and go away and you won't pay much notice. It comes up again, lasts a little longer, goes away, and you still don't see it as alarming. "It's normal," "It's only temporary," you tell yourself. Then one day you realize it has come and hasn't gone, you're well into the cortisol, the Symptoms are overwhelming and sobriety is in danger. Gradually you adapt to the stressors until they reach a crisis point. It's similar to experiments of which I've heard (but have too much heart to prove on my own) where a frog will die or hop out if tossed into 100 degree water but will swim in a pot of cold water placed on a burner right up until the point where the water boils. You adapt and adapt to the stressors until suddenly you're at a boiling point.

The stressors we pile up over periods of sobriety aren't the small day-by-day stressors like coffee spills on new carpet. They're the four major category stressors covered in chapters four through seven.

The longer you spend in prolonged stress with the cortisol rioting through you, the more intense your feelings of helplessness and, sometimes, emotional numbness. You at times feel like you're just going through the motions. Adrenals, like the rest of the body, are not designed for prolonged stress according to Dr. Aphrodite Matsakis (*I Can't Get Over It*, New Harbinger Publications, Oakland, CA 1992). "The adrenals can be permanently damaged leading to overfunctioning during subsequent stress. If you were subjected to repeated or intense trauma or stress, certain biochemicals may have been depleted."

In a famous series of experiments conducted by Martin Seligman in the 1970s, animals were subjected to electrical shocks they could not flee no matter what they did or did not do (*Helplessness: On Depression, Development and Death*, W.H. Freeman, San Francisco, CA 1975). They fought at first. Later the animals became listless when shocked. This was phase one. In Seligman's second phase, the animals were shocked again but could prevent the zap by pressing a button. They didn't. They were too changed biochemically to take a simple action to end their suffering. Bessel van der Kolk (in *Journal of Traumatic Stress*, Vol. 1, 1988) followed up the Seligman work and concluded the shocked creatures had the same biochemical imbalances as humans enduring prolonged exposure to stressors. With people though, human nature dictates that we try to avoid or escape anything to do with the stressor. Someone might, for example, avoid driving a car after the stress of a car wreck. That is a single, short-duration stressor. An Alcoholic, like Seligman's experiment subjects, has multiple stressors of long duration. And you can't run from them all. Like the two experiments convincingly demonstrated, there's a point at which we don't even save ourselves.

Initially as we begin abstinence, we're told to save ourselves from triggers. People. Places. Things. And the things in slogan-happy and acronym-rich rehab we call HALT: being Hungry, Angry, Lonely or Tired. Research demonstrates that those triggers lead to lapse because you are not thinking your clearest thoughts. When your stomach growls the oldest parts of the brain focus your body's resources on food. If you're focused on food, you're not focused on sobriety, the thinking goes. You're juggling sobriety's apples and hunger throws you a chainsaw. When you're tired, your thinking is blunted by your need for sleep. When you're angry or lonely, you may prioritize resolving those emotions rather than concentrating on sobriety. HALT is a good starting point. The objective is to stay out of harm's way. Avoid. But the major stressors knocking our cortisol out of whack and leading to lapse, you cannot avoid.
Psychiatrists Thomas Holmes and Richard Rahe of the University of Washington School of Medicine developed an inventory of major stressors that can be used to identify the things that can lead to the Symptoms of Sobriety. Scientists began using this scale to understand the relationship between stressors and illnesses ranging from cancer to the common cold ("Social Readjustment Rating Scale," *Journal of Psychosomatic Research*, Vol. 11 Issue 2 1967).

Social Readjustment Rating Scale

Event	Value (each time)	Event	Value (each time)
1. Death of spouse	100	23. Child leaving home	29
2. Divorce	73	24. In-law trouble	29
3. Separation	65	25. Win an award	28
4. Jail	63	26. Spouse starts/stops work	26
5. Death in family	63	27. Start/stop school	26
6. Major illness (Alcoholism)	53	28. Construction at home	25
7. Marriage	50	29. Change in personal habits	24
8. Being fired	47	30. Trouble with boss	23
9. Marital reconciliation	45	31. Change in work conditions/hours	20
10. Retirement	45	32. Moving	20
11. Major change in family health	45	33. Changing schools	20
12. Pregnancy	40	34. Change in amt./type of recreation	19
13. Sexual difficulties	39	35. Change in church attendance	19
14. New member in household	39	36. Change in social activity	19
15. Business change (reorg.)	39	37. Taking on a loan	17
16. Financial status change	38	38. Change in sleep habits	16
17. Death of close friend	37	39. Change in family gathering freq.	15
18. Job change	36	40. Change in eating habits	15
19. Increase/decrease in arguing	35	41. Vacation	13
20. New mortgage	31	42. Christmas	12
21. Foreclosure	30	43 Traffic tickets	11
22. Promotion/demotion	29		

Total your scores from the scale. A total of 150-300 is excessive. For non-Alcoholics. Above 300 is severe. If you're Alcoholic, *automatically* score at least 96 just walking around. You have a disease (#6), you have REM sleep disruption (#38), your caloric intake is suspect (#40), and if you're Christian you have Christmas (#42). The scale ignores daily stressors, our most frequent hassles, which don't ratchet up the cortisol of so-called normal people. The top five of these daily, minor stressors according to Allen D. Kanner ("Comparison of Two Modes of Stress Measurement," *Journal of Behavioral Medicine*, 1981):

My weight/my looks
Cost of common good
Housework/yardwork
Misplaced/lost things
And a tie between crime and Property/investments/taxes

According to Kanner this is the small stuff, the buttered-toast-always-falls-face-down, temporary hassles which give us a minor shock or sensation but we quickly regain our balance. With the bigger stressors from the scale, we're stuck and don't regain the balance as promptly. Walter Cannon (*The Wisdom of the Body*, WC Norton, New York 1932) called our balance homeostasis and concluded 80 years ago that some of us deplete our resources after a major stressor without regaining our homeostasis. "Prolonged exposure to prolonged severe absence of homeostasis leads eventually to a breakdown in our biological system." He was referring to your faulty cortisol response as an example of the breakdown stemming from prolonged stress.

Combining Cannon's work with that of Hans Seyle, who also studied how our bodies fend off toxicity and illness ("General Adaptation Syndrome" in *Stress Without Distress*, New American Library, New York 1979), with what we now know about cortisol gives us the following graphic representation of how stressors impact balance and sobriety.

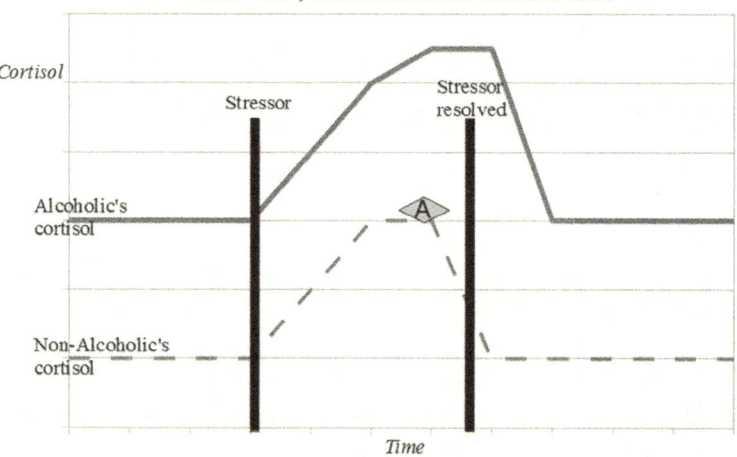

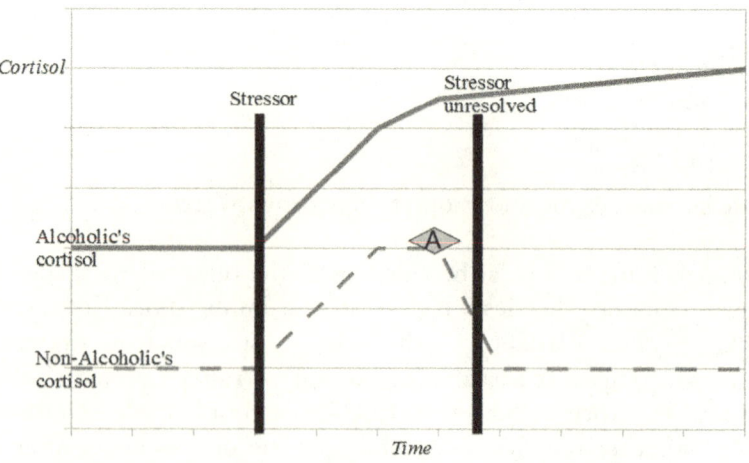

Ⓐ Non-Alcoholic's cortisol is depleted, whether or not a stressor is resolved

You'll notice boredom isn't on the scale, isn't in Kanner's short list of daily stressors and isn't part of HALT triggers. Boredom is not a real stressor, but a reaction to stressors. When we aren't satisfied, we're bored. And we might get the feeling we need to shake things up a bit by trying to make a change listed on the scale. Change for the sake of change is not a clever thing to do when you fear the Symptoms of Sobriety. If you're already at or over 150 on the scale, you're jeopardizing your recovery just to cure boredom. If an Alcoholic says he's bored, that's a statement with more bullshit than a rodeo. It's a warning that another stressor is causing him dissatisfaction. It could be trouble, or it could simply be a sign that he's spending way too much time thinking about himself.

There are four additional major stressors around which this book was built. They don't make the list of individual events on the scale, but are the cortisol-spiking foundations of the Symptoms of Sobriety. The four are not unique to Alcoholics. Anyone can experience them, however they are extreme barriers to relapse prevention because of our already high base of cortisol and already high scores on a stress scale. After my lapse and before researching the cortisol connection I asked more than 280 other men and women who had a lapse to think beyond the HALT triggers and the daily stress to find what things were agitating them in the month or so predating the lapse. I just didn't want to lapse again myself, so my methodology is admittedly informal, but the results were consistent. They weren't prompted or given a list from which to choose, but consistently came up with the same four categories.

For those on the outside of the disease, in a way, dealing with a drinking Alcoholic is easier than dealing with a sober one because with a drinking one you *know* what the problem is. The conversations I had reveal what the sober Alcoholic's problems are.

When the Symptoms of Sobriety appear, know they are normal responses to cortisol increase traced to these four things we struggle with in sobriety:

Guilt (Chapter Four)
Shame (Chapter Five)
Forgiveness (Chapter Six)
Grief (Chapter Seven)

When you take away alcohol you still have problems—problems that non-Alcoholics sometimes use alcohol to relieve, "treat" or cover up. In an Alcoholic, these four cause relapse. They are the cloud to sobriety's silver

33

lining. They aren't simply squishy, intangible emotional qualities for Hallmark cards or spiritual books. Science shows they're states that have a concrete and measurable effect on our biochemistry.

Every Alcoholic has manifestations of these four and needs treatment geared toward these stressors or the treatment fails. No treatment will have lasting success without addressing what causes the Symptoms of Sobriety. To put it another way, it's well known that high cholesterol levels increase coronary heart disease—heart trouble. Those who have a genetic predisposition for difficulty handling cholesterol frequently can forestall heart trouble with careful eating habits. A person who doesn't have the problem handling cholesterol doesn't have the same urgent need to restrict his diet. Eating ice cream or gorging on fries isn't much of an issue for him but it is for the man who does have the genetic predisposition. And so it goes with Alcoholics who are stuck with a problem handling cortisol. Guilt, shame, forgiveness and grief are a threat to recovery trouble like cholesterol is a threat to heart trouble.

Chapter Three

> *"You can tell what a man thinks about living by what he thinks about death."*—Dag Hammerskjold

Cortisol is the explanation for feeling the Symptoms but it is not an excuse for that drink or other drastic measures. Things can seem *really* drastic, too. Without addressing the stressors the way later chapters suggest, just how dramatically can excess cortisol influence you, your thoughts and behaviors? Well, lapse is one drastic outcome, as I stunningly demonstrated. Outwardly I appeared to be doing so well at the time and obviously I wasn't since I relapsed, but that wasn't even close to how decayed I felt. The clarity I was showing everyone was an illusion. The clarity of my thinking was so distorted by the Symptoms that two weeks following my lapse, despite all this "serenity" so many thought I had just weeks prior, I decided to take my life before my sentence was over. Some serenity. Albert Camus said, "The only serious question is whether to kill yourself or not." Shitty question, Al. And my equally shitty chemistry told me the answer was, "Yeah, I should." It wasn't an impulse decision of that day (Halloween coincidentally). I carried that plan for weeks, built on thoughts poisoned by cortisol. To know the imbalance and pain of such a decision is to know sadness few live to tell about. And they say *alcohol* messes up your thoughts? This was cortisol. I had no alcohol in me when I decided I had to die. I found my bottom, without a drop of Jack Daniel's in me.

There's a lot of banter in counseling circles about hitting your bottom. The bottom for me wasn't any of the dark days mentioned in my previous book, like hitting a BAC of .612 or being jailed or losing money/family/freedoms/friendships. The bottom was losing hope October 31. The Symptoms of Sobriety brought me to a bottom met without an ounce of alcohol in me. The furious, non-stop, ravenous, two-liters-a-day maintenance drinking days

I ended more than three years earlier had no bottom like this. I didn't find a bottom while swimming in alcohol, I hit it swimming in cortisol while stone sober.

The Symptoms made me feel as though I wanted to die at times over the preceding years of sobriety, but now I actually wanted to kill myself. There's a huge gulf of a difference between wanting to die and actually planning it. Wanting to die just means you're sick of feeling like hell, but being suicidal means you're actively doing something about it regardless of how it would crush everyone around you.

I always gave myself credit for knowing better than to think such thoughts of life being so disposable. I know with certainty that millions of people struggle with worse things than the legal mess I created and never even think about killing themselves. Yet here I was on the brink anyway because the Symptoms had so overwhelmed all that good sense. I wanted to die. I wrote in my journal a few days later, "My mind is made up." I was done. Done losing after all the sober months. My confidence was gone as was my optimism and my laughter. The Symptoms won and I was quitting.

I wrote the letter next. I still have it today. It reads something like this: Me, me, me.

I still remember the elaborate plans I had to construct to carry it out. It's not easy to pull off while incarcerated. The only thing more difficult than killing yourself in jail is getting helped out of such unclear thoughts. (I contacted their social worker four times over sixty days without the courtesy of a single reply. Meanwhile she was twice spotted on weekday newscasts among the protestors at the state capitol.)

I still recall vividly the day I called it off, killing my plan rather than killing myself. January 6. I remembered the tree of sorrows parable I mentioned at the end of my last book . . . how at the end of life we gather our dark days and sorrows and place them on a tree and are given an opportunity to take instead someone else's sorrows from the tree, yet every man chooses to keep his own rather than another's batch of sorrows. The tree seemed bigger, the sorrows heavier, than when I put that in my previous book, but on January 6 I realized my own sorrows were what I was supposed to keep. What happens sometimes when facing suicide is that a person realizes what they hate about living can be fixed. So they call it off. Some sort of optimism reawakens. Not so with me. There wasn't a prosthetic optimism. I called it off because I still saw what

I hated about living couldn't be fixed, but the lives of my kids would be even worse. Their visit to a tree of sorrows would be a leaden one if their sorrows included their dad's selfish death. My guilt—my main stressor but far from my only one—was a disgraceful rationale for taking away my kids' dad or to have my mom bury a son. Pitying myself over how lousy the guilt made me feel made me lose sight of how really lucky I was. It was time to find out how much shock absorber I had left in me.

For eight or nine more months afterward I still struggled with figuring out why sobriety wasn't such a silver lining, but I was done trying to take my life over it. It's said that those who've come close to death often use the second chance at life to redeem earlier mistakes or to seek meaning in their remaining years. Uncovering the Symptoms and the connection to the four stressors in sobriety is how I decided to move to January 7 with meaning.

I also read something from Eleanor Roosevelt that motivated me to dig in, to live, and to begin to research what brought me to this bottom. The passage from Roosevelt appeared in *You Learn By Living* (Westminster Press, Philadelphia 1983). "Though you think at the time [a situation] is impossible and you go through the tortures of the damned, once you have met it and lived through it you find that forever after you are freer than you were before." A great quote . . . not even the one Roosevelt or the book is known for, but taken on its own it is good. Taken in the context of my frame of mind those days, it was profoundly moving and seemed as if those words were spoken directly to me so I'd look to uncover answers to the Symptoms and the stressors behind them.

Chapter Four

"One need not be a chamber to be haunted."—Emily Dickinson

The first of the four stressors that stimulate the cortisol condition in Alcoholics is guilt. It's not guilt over some things we've done wrong. Sooner or later we forgive ourselves for these peccadilloes. If we don't we find ourselves lapsing before getting too far into sobriety because, as the eponymous AA book says, "We will never get over drinking until we have done our utmost to straighten out the past." The old incidents, while stressful, are not a major stressor and usually are well into our rearview mirrors by the time we're into sobriety a few months. Instead, this stressor refers to the guilt an Alcoholic carries—or buries—about *having Alcoholism.*

The concept of guilt isn't exclusive to Alcoholism, nor does guilt grow suddenly out of abstinence. Instead, the guilt has seeds in the soil of our Terrible Twos. We grew from being a baby, where we could be physically controlled by our parents by a playpen or crib if we went where they didn't care for us to be, to being an impetuous and obstinate and verbal creature of two where the playpen and physical control didn't work as well.

We were taught right from wrong at that age as the parents used psychological control to replace physical control. In psychological control, our mom's say, "That's a good boy" (or girl) when we do something as asked of us instead of plopping us into playpens when they're no longer practical. The same mom will tell us we're bad for tracking in mud or we're disappointing for not cleaning up our rooms or we're naughty for slugging the neighbor kid. Guilt was a conditioning tool, a training method, to control our behavior and to begin teaching us how to live around others without making them want to strangle us. That's really all moms are trying to do with all these "shoulds:"

Keep their offspring from physical harm today and later on in life. There's no malice intended . . . but here guilt is born.

Please note I'm saying "mom" only because we do spend most of our early childhood and especially the Terrible Twos in mom's care, not dad's, but dad does this training, too, and neither are doing it out of anything but love.

Guilt also proved to be a good teacher of values and of respect. For example, I grew up in a home of Catholic values and as a result I not only had guilt from the parenting control I also had the Big Guy With The Long White Beard to contend with. Add in the TV of the 1970s that brought the globe into our living rooms and heightened other social values. We now had to eat our carrots because mom said it was right, God wanted us to eat them and there were kids starving in Ethiopia. Another favorite example of how guilt works as control: "Are *your* legs broken?" is a guilt-inducing response when you ask mom to come, "Come here." *How could you dare* ask mom to, "Come here," when you were capable of walking *to* the grown up. Why would you make her suffer the walk? What kind of kid makes such demands? Guilt is an efficient teacher of respect and structure in that regard. This blueprint for social interaction, for doing what's right, is like luggage. You keep it forever.

You learn what was right or naughty or disappointing because you did it. From the Terrible Twos on you associate wrong with mom's voice and mood. The tone told you something scary or unpleasant will happen to you. Mom attached emotionally loaded ideas like wrong and right to your *actions* and something *you* did. Like tracking mud in or slugging that neighbor. She did it to help control and to teach responsibility. You don't have to find the taste of aspirin agreeable to see it helps your headache, nor do you have to agree with psychological control to see it works. Children from lousy parenting have no concept of guilt because they've missed this chapter of their training, so while some criticize good boy/bad boy psychological lessons as manipulative, the value gained by growing a conscience and a concept of guilt in this fashion outstrips any benefit of not conditioning kids to respect right and rights. We've all seen kids who grew into adult bodies without ever having heard, "No!" and without learning important boundaries or guilt. That is, of course, if you are capable of guilt. Caltech and University of Iowa researchers in 2011 identified a region of the brain (ventromedial prefrontal cortex) as the guilt locker of the brain. If through injury or birth defect this part of your grey matter doesn't have an on-switch you don't feel guilt. The word for most people unable to feel guilt because of shoddy parenting or this type of injury: Sociopath.

Your training in guilt comes from your parents. They got it from theirs. And so on. Spock or Gesell or Patterson were great theorists on raising kids, but when the real world happens, we go with what we learned from the way we were brought up ourselves and guilt works.

Think about the high school yearbook. If you have one—and you're in a *graduating* class—you achieved a social milestone and a respectable right of passage because you had been subjected to this humility, this psychological training, and a homeopathic dose of guilt in your formative years. Good parenting . . . good guilt. A value was instilled in you that it was important or "right" to graduate. Now a diploma is no guarantee that you're tethered to any moral compass, but if you don't have the senior class picture and dropped out, you probably never got that homeopathic guilt injection that graduation was "right" (or you improvised with your own set of more convenient shoulds and rights to combat the guilt). Alcoholics have a yearbook in the brain that is missing the picture of themselves in the graduating class and feel a painful guilt for not living up to the idea that they should be in one.

So guilt in and of itself is not a bad thing. In fact, *some* guilt is homeopathic. It preserves a barrier between barbaric thoughts and behaviors and keeps us humble. Homeopathic guilt is what we call "scruples" or "scrupulousness" and we call those without, "unscrupulous." We're born without a single scruple. (Think of how unscrupulous the demands of an infant can seem . . . wonderful and precious but unscrupulous as hell.) We acquire scruples and humility through this training program of our parents.

Who can argue with humility in small doses? It's the larger servings we serve ourselves in recovery that lead to our cortisol issues and the Symptoms of Sobriety because somewhere between the Terrible Twos and our teens, we also learned that Alcoholism was on the half of the ledger marked "wrong" and we feel wrong for having it.

Alcoholics pile upon this foundation of guilt a collection of things we actually did, things we failed to do and a menagerie of doings that violate a bunch of other arbitrary things we were brought up to believe were right. We grow a cloud over our heads when we're drinking of things we should be doing. Then when we sober up, we regret or resent that we didn't live up to them. When the alcohol is gone, we begin a struggle with the guilt over those wrongs and the wrong we feel we've committed just for having this disease. We try to prove we're not wrong; we're not disappointing. That cloud of our miscues and forgotten humility can feel like it is following us constantly, and that leads to the Symptoms because we cannot outrun our cloud of guilt.

The classic, *Sophie's Choice*, by William Styron, demonstrates how the cloud of guilt can overwhelm when we create it from conflicts with our values. In the story, Sophie is forced by Nazis to chose which of her children will die immediately and which will live. If she doesn't make a choice, both children will be killed. Sophie made a choice and lived with a cloud of guilt over her for the rest of her life until it leads to her tragic death. Did she really *have* a choice in her situation? One or both children were going to die . . . pick one? Does an Alcoholic choose Alcoholism? You get to have it or you don't? It's a genetic package, not a choice. Sophie doesn't die if she faces down her guilt over a choice that really was no choice. Alcoholics aren't doomed to failure if they face down their guilt over a choice that really was no choice.

The first cloud of guilt for the Alcoholic in sobriety comes from if we've physically hurt someone. That doesn't apply to all of us. The second cloud is over other ways we've victimized people emotionally, financially, socially and/or psychologically. Once you're away from the booze awhile you discover these hurts are far bigger than broken bones and that you've created more pain and more victims than you realized. You broke so many of those values with which you were raised. And you realize all those people you had fooled weren't really fooled at all.

We pile on all these clouds over things we "should have" done based upon how we were brought up. We live under a "Tyranny of Shoulds," a term coined by Freudian psychoanalyst Karen Horney (*Neurosis and Human Growth*, Norton, New York 1950). All the things we should be or should have done but alcohol came first. We box ourselves in rigidly with these irrational shoulds from our drinking days. On top of that box we slam a lid of things we should be doing in sobriety: I should never make mistakes now that I'm sober . . . I should never be afraid now . . . I should always be busy . . . I should not feel hurt by the disease or by others . . . I should now behave like the perfect citizen/dad/husband . . . I should be the walking definition of unselfishness. The guilt over the old shoulds at which we failed and the new sobriety shoulds we try to keep up is a stress. It's irrational. Eighteenth century philosopher Edmund Burke opined, "Guilt is never a rational thing. It distorts all the faculties of the human mind, it perverts them, it leaves a man no longer in the free use of his reason, it puts him in confusion." Confusion . . . one of the Symptoms.

The danger of shoulding also is mentioned prominently in the work of Albert Ellis on the relationship between events and feelings. Ellis was not involved in alcohol treatment but his work set the foundation for Self-Management and Recovery Training (SMART), an alternative to 12-step recovery. Ellis reasons that we feel guilt not because of what happens but because of beliefs we have about the events before they happen, an idea borrowed from first century Greek philosopher Epictetus. Ellis says four basic irrational beliefs are at the core of all guilt we feel. One of them is "what I believe I should or should not do," the unwritten laws we give ourselves. (Albert Ellis and Robert Harper, *A Guide to Rational Living*, Wilshire Book Company, Chatsworth, CA 1961) Shoulds amount to an evaluation *of yourself* based on a list of beliefs you began creating when your parents first exercised their psychological control over you. The way we evaluate things and ourselves as good/bad, true/untrue, etc. goes back to our toddler years. Think about how you feel about snakes. What age were you when you got the belief they were creepy (or cool)? Where did you learn that? From mom who also thought snakes were creepy (or cool). Did you develop that evaluation rationally? Smoking. Hallmark holidays. TV. Love. Broccoli. Fast food. Grandma's cooking. Alcohol. All of these things have beliefs attached to them, beliefs we assigned from a very early age.

The following 10 statements from Ellis's work form the foundation of most, if not all, our guilt:

1. I need everyone's love and approval.
2. I should do everything well.
3. If something bad happens I should worry about it.
4. It is easier to avoid things than to risk failure.
5. I'll enjoy life more if I avoid responsibility in favor of what I can take here and now.
6. Some people are bad and deserve to be punished.
7. When things aren't going well, my life is a disaster.
8. If things go wrong, I have to be able to fix it.
9. What happened before will happen again and the same way.
10. Perfect solutions should be available for everything.

When these 10 statements manage you, you have guilt. That's Ellis' take. Other psychologists refer to his top ten and guilt in general as "negative self-talk." In fact, one of the top-selling pop-psychology self-help books of all time, Norman Vincent Peale's *The Power of Positive Thinking*, is dedicated to overcoming negative self-talks. Neither Peale nor Ellis wrote specifically about guilt as it relates to Alcoholism. Nor did they know the connection between cortisol and guilt back then. Today we do know how guilt and Alcoholism and cortisol are knitted together.

It's garbage-in, garbage-out: We had erroneous messaging about Alcoholism inserted into our beliefs in early childhood, messaging that was based on naïve, misinformed stereotypes of Alcoholism. And now we batter ourselves over those irrational beliefs. Guilt, therefore, is a condition we arrive at when our values collide with our reality, our actions and our disease. When I was 10, my parents were splitting up. My father, a regional sales rep, was a weekend dad even before the divorce because of his job. Since he was in his car throughout his territory five days a week, he had a CB radio. It was a 70's thing. He gave me a walkie talkie tuned to a CB channel so I could talk to him while he was still within range before or after his visits. I'd climb to the landing at the top of the stairs in our old stone house and use the radio by the window to stretch out the reception as long as possible. When the radio static crackled his voice away into the Sunday night, that spot at the top of the stairs became the Loneliest Spot in America. As I became a dad, I swore I would do all I could to keep my own children from discovering another Loneliest Spot in America. That was my top value, one formed in my childhood. "A dad *should* be there." Because I failed early and often in handling what alcohol was doing to my life and my kids' lives, I became the voice my own kids couldn't hear during the months in treatment or jail. I created a Loneliest Spot in America. That's my guilt. My values collided with my reality. And their's.

We may have started with the values imposed upon us in our Terrible Twos or built from childhood lessons, but don't blame the parenting. We are capable of resetting the values we assign illness in general and Alcoholism specifically. If we don't, if we're still bent around those early values, we subject ourselves to the cortisol difficulty that goes along with guilt.

Do the values require resetting? According to psychologists Sidney Simon, Leland Howe and Howard Kushenbaum (*Values Clarification*, Warner Books, New York 1995) a value isn't a value unless it has these factors: It must be freely chosen; It must be chosen from a consideration of other alternatives; It must be chosen with clear knowledge of consequences; It must be prized and cherished; It must be admitted or spoken, and; It must be acted upon repeatedly. You're going to be in conflict if, for example, you admit you are Alcoholic but also learned in your childhood belief #6 on Ellis's list (Some people are bad and deserved to be punished) and were told back then that Alcoholics were bad people. Yet these "values" don't even pass the first test above: You didn't freely choose the values, they were imposed upon you.

Somewhere along the long history of Alcoholism it became wrong to blame the disease instead of the person. That's faulty thinking that lurks behind guilt. The disease is a biological condition that manages its carrier. The disease is the bad guy, not you. If a fight broke between guests in your home, it isn't the home's fault or your fault. It's the guests'. Blame is an important part of combatting guilt. Fritz Heider identifies levels of responsibility for blame (*The Psychology of Interpersonal Relations*, Lawrence Erlbaum Inc., Hillside, NJ 1958). Level one—did you contribute? Level two—was it foreseeable? Level three—was it intentional? ==Alcoholism is never intentional. Of what are you guilty?==

You may think that mentally beating yourself up for not getting help, not getting it sooner or for having the disease at all will motivate you to live up to your potential. That's not accurate according to counselor Robin Casarjian (*Houses of Healing*, Lionheart Press, Boston 1995). "Chronically unhealthy guilt and self-blame can seem to serve as a constant nagging that we need to wake ourselves up, yet when we don't live up the next time guilt is actually keeping the power to heal ourselves inactive" by creating even more guilt. It's called a squirrel cage, a concept covered in the next chapter.

An enormous amount has been written about the psychology of guilt in the second half of the last century. *Guilt: Letting Go*, by Lucy Freeman and Dr. Herbert Strean (John Wiley & Sons, New York 1986) is among the best. By comparison, this chapter is succinct because ==Alcoholics only need to recognize guilt as a stressor that blisters everyone with the disease==. I'm merely pointing to the fact that Alcoholics have it and the sensation or experience of guilt places you at a vulnerable spot in recovery when it is ignored. Like the dark side of the moon, it may be out of sight, but it is always there.

Guilt is unlike the other three stressors because guilt is an entirely subjective experience, one felt individually and uniquely. Like if you stubbed your toe, you feel the pain and nobody else feels it the same way at the same time, on the same toe or at the same intensity. You have your own scale for intensity, too. You didn't stub the hardened toe of a soccer pro, who would have a different idea of the pain. The sensation of guilt is different for each of us. We all have it though. Whether it is over having the disease or for the chaos we left in our wakes.

Since family is nearest, Alcoholics feel much guilt about them or around them for a couple of reasons. First, there's guilt over how we treated them. No Alcoholic is exempt: We all treated family to a show (a disgustingly poor one at times). We hurt them and alienated them. An Alcoholic brushes the teeth of his own worst enemy every morning but never counted on brushing the teeth of his family's worst enemy. Even if they have never said as much, you feel you've made enemies out of them and feel guilty over it. In time this guilt fades as the memories become history the longer we're sober. Second, there's guilt over creating co-dependents (once called co-Alcoholics) because there's an evil myth that's persisted for decades that Alcoholics *cause* co-dependence.

You didn't cause co-dependence and cannot blame yourself for a family member's co-dependence. You only gave them an object. They were sick before your disease and it is a separate, unique disorder.

Al-Anon came about in the 1950s as a reflex of AA. It's the largest, most well-known co-dependent support group and does spend a ton of energy on how to live with an Alcoholic. Al-Anon's close link to Alcoholics is no doubt the source of the erroneous conclusion that the condition of co-dependency is exclusively a phenomenon related to or caused by Alcoholism. However, co-dependence is a condition separate from the disease, says Anne Wilson-Schaef in *Co-Dependence: Misunderstood—Mistreated* (Harper & Row, New York 1986). "It's an illness in its own right that involves an Alcoholic but could just as easily involve a compulsive eater or gambler" in the Alcoholic's place and would have if you hadn't happened along. Co-dependence is a pre-existing condition that emerges after prolonged contact and close association with anyone who has *any* physical illness or mental compulsion. If Alcoholism means depending on alcohol at the risk of all else, co-dependency means depending on relationships above all else. Not specifically Alcoholics, but other human beings, too. Co-dependents are addicted to people. It's just usually addicted people they chose as objects. Psychologists call them "external referenting," which simply means all their self-worth comes from other people. By the way, this is the most common characteristic of co-dependence.

You don't even have to ask the co-dependent to give themselves up like that. They just do it without being asked. And it's hard to not blame ourselves for their sacrifice and feel guilty over it.

Psychologist Robert Subby was one of Wilson-Schaef's contemporaries in the mid-80s when recognition of co-dependency began to gain momentum. In *Co-Dependency: An Emerging Issue* (Health Communications, Pompano Beach, FL 1984), Subby is very direct about the relationship to Alcoholism. "Co-dependency is a behavior pattern of copy that is born not as a result of Alcoholism." You have no reason to feel guilt over it.

In 2011, the tendency for a person to become co-dependent was shown to have a biological source, oxytocin, just like Alcoholism is traced to neurochemicals dopamine and serotonin and lapse is connected to cortisol. Oxytocin is a compound related to a person's nurturing response to others. Co-dependents and others with a greater capacity for empathy were found to have more of a certain type of oxytocin receptor (type GG) compared to less empathetic humans, who have more type AG or type AA receptors. I know, that's too much geek speak for me, too, so I'm not going further into the science than that. The problem isn't you; the co-dependent is just wired that way.

We define co-dependence by its three stages of progression:

1. Normal problem solving skews ... as a reaction to reduce the family crisis and ease the Alcoholic's pain. This *is* sick thinking because it ignores the fact that a non-Alcoholic is powerless to control an Alcoholic's disease. As the Alcoholic becomes increasingly preoccupied with getting, using and keeping booze, the co-dependent becomes more focused on him and begins to change her own behavior in response to the Alcoholic's lifestyle. (I use "her" because co-dependents often are female, there are males, too. I know several, including myself.)
2. Self-defeating problem solving emerges . . . after the previous stage fails to achieve any progress the co-dependent tries *harder*. Here's where a co-dependent becomes more obvious since they begin to take responsibility for the Alcoholic and does so at the cost of their own needs. Behavior may switch from trying to check on or control the drinker and keeping peace in the family to isolation from activities outside the family. They're not as aware of how they feel but can go on and on about how the Alcoholic feels.
3. Chronic repetition takes over . . . regardless of the health of the Alcoholic (e.g. whether they are using, abstaining or in recovery) the co-dependent keeps tending to the Alcoholic because doing so has become her identity. A co-dependent doubts anyone would want them around otherwise, so she makes herself indispensable to the drinker. She'll struggle when you get well because by stopping drinking you've removed from her the single way she made herself indispensable. Minding the Alcoholic has become the meaning of her existence and she needs the Alcoholic to be sick for her to feel well.

That last sentence is a huge source of guilt and conflict, and an ironic one at that, because you can feel guilty for getting better if it seems to be making her worse. You see her struggle with co-dependence even after you've had some measure of sobriety. She doesn't seem to function well or at all without the drinking you. The quality of her life depends upon how much you need her and you feel guilt over that.

There's no denying that co-dependents feel pain. Sometimes it's even physical, usually gastrointestinal problems. Guilt is misplaced if you believe you're to blame. The condition with the oxytocin was there before you were sick.

An Alcoholic isn't sicker than the co-dependent. You are both struggling with similar issues in dissimilar ways. In some ways, the co-dependent is trying to deal with your issues for you. Or attempting to. Dr. Charles Whitfield suggests the hallmark of co-dependency is a problem with boundaries and not knowing where she ends and you begin. "Co-dependents cannot develop without distortions in personal boundaries." (*Co-Dependence: Healing the Human Condition*, Health Communications, Deerfield Beach, FL 1991) He didn't say co-dependents cannot develop without an Alcoholic.

Every Alcoholic's road back to health begins with an aha! moment when he realizes, "I *have* an alcohol problem." A co-dependent needs to have her own aha! moment to realize she has a disorder. Her self-identifying is part of *her* process of healing and discovering she's not sick like you or sick from you. You're not the right person to give her the a-ha moment. Her own lemons; her own lemonade. There's Al-Anon or Co-Dependents Anonymous (CoDA) or counseling for her. You cannot rescue her just like NO ONE could rescue you. You can help her. You can't be her. You make piles, just like sorting laundry. Colors vs. whites. Your hurts vs. hers. Your disease vs. her disorder. What you can help vs. what you cannot. Don't wash her red shirt with your white towels. Have empathy. Show you care . . . which you can do without guilting yourself. The best tribute you can pay to her is to pay attention to your sobriety and its Symptoms.

In no way am I suggesting you cannot recover with or around co-dependents. You can and will. Just be mindful that in early sobriety you are not the safest people for one another and the outlook is weak. A sick home or family can make you sicker faster than a whole army of doctors can make you well. I mean dangerously sicker, because your disease is fatal and the co-dependency disorder isn't. It's not likely they'll actually encourage you to drink. That can happen but isn't common. It's usually not so sinister. Instead, it's vastly more probable the guilt you generate inside will pile up from living in close proximity to your co-dependent, leading to the Symptoms and increasing your risk of lapse. Later, in both recoveries, the emotional investment you have in one another is a plus and outweighs the dangers from early sobriety. In fact, according to Wilson-Schaef, "It's accurately believed that Alcoholics have less chance to lapse if they return to treated families who no longer practice their co-dependence."

Her healing can be as lengthy as yours. It could take three to five years. And just like your own recovery, there is no finish line.

If we were dealing with broken bones, it would be so much easier.

Here's an unexpected kicker. According to one of the earliest pioneers of co-dependent behavior research, Sharon Wegshieder-Cruse ("Co-Dependency," Nurturing Networks Inc., St. Paul, MN 1984), recovering Alcoholics are at the greatest risk of becoming a co-dependent. As if you didn't have enough with which to contend in recovery: You're addicted to alcohol, and now you run the risk of becoming addicted to the well-being of those you terrorized. You want to compensate for the damage you did as a drinker and the pendulum can and often does swing back too far. Whitfield agrees with Wegshieder-Cruse on the risk. "In decades of work, I've never seen an Alcoholic who is not also a co-dependent."

It's because of the guilt.

There are still more issues surrounding recovering around your family. They include: Scapegoating personal and family problems onto the Alcoholic; and creating unrealistic expectations for how dramatically family life will improve once you've been sober awhile. These are two great destroyers of family unity and of sobriety. They may feel like guilt, but when you squeeze the water out of them, they look like shame instead.

Chapter Five

"The judge is condemned when the guilty party is acquitted."—*Publilius Syrus*

One of the first TV newsrooms in which I worked had an old-school assignment editor who had above his desk a framed photo from his reporter days. He was on the Patty Hearst story in California. In the 1970s, the newspaper heiress was kidnapped by a violent left-wing activist group that forced the 19-year-old into a role in a series of crimes for which she was put on trial in '79. The photo shows her outside the court in a t-shirt that read, "Being kidnapped is always having to say you're sorry." Drop kidnapped and insert Alcoholic and that shirt could communicate how it sometimes feels when you're working toward recovery. First, a violent abduction from your day-to-day life makes you a hostage, then your guilt and shame subject you to years of feeling as though you won't ever be able to atone for it.

Guilt and shame are different. Psychiatrist Helen Block Lewis points out, "Shame and guilt often occur together. They're frequently fused and therefore confused with each other." (*The Role of Shame in Symptom Formation*, Lawrence Erlbaum Inc., Hillside, NJ 1987) Shame is the feeling *we get from others* that we *are* wrong . . . guilt is the feeling *we give ourselves* when we *do* wrong. In guilt, you're reviewing your own irrational beliefs and telling yourself you didn't do enough and you punish yourself for it . . . in shame, someone else is saying you didn't do enough based on their own irrational beliefs. The former is caused by your values . . . the latter is caused by others imposing their values on you. The gap between your performance and your expectations of yourself is guilt . . . the gap between your performance and others' expectations of you is shame. When you feel guilt over being Alcoholic, you feel the disease has made you a monster . . . when you feel shame, other people behave as if you *are* a monster.

As for their impact on cortisol, guilt and shame have the same outcome even though their origins are so different. The cortisol doesn't make a distinction between whether others are judging you or you are judging yourself. The judgment is that Alcoholism is not "normal."

The words that can derail sobriety more than any others are: You're Not Normal. Not You Are Dying or You're An Alcoholic or I Want A Divorce or You're Fired. You're Not Normal is a judgment that impacts your cortisol like a supernova. Shame—the Master Emotion—carries that kind of whallop.

Our society sucks if you consider how judgmental and completely arbitrary we are about what is normal. Need an illustration? Think of how full of praise we are when we come across someone who is kind in only a general sort of way, not a Mother Theresa sort of way, because kindness isn't normal anymore. We gush over good Samaritans and secret Santas even though as the higher species on this rock those are the ways we should be treating people every day. We're generally okay to one another, but we are at our worst not with our fists or weapons but with our words of shame for people who don't fit "normal."

Just like a little guilt can be homeopathic, so, too, is a little shame. Say a neighbor puts down the upkeep of my house. I feel ashamed and fix it up and move on. Or, if I internalize his put down, I'll fix the house and keep fixing it because I feel I am a terrible homeowner. Finally I bankrupt my accounts and probably want to burn his house down. Extreme? Sure. But we Alcoholics bankrupt our self-image when we internalize shame over other people's naïve view of the disease. Shame *internalized* isn't homeopathic, it is toxic to the Alcoholic.
Jean Paul Sartre's famed quote, "Hell. It is other people," stands as a good theme for this stressor, but other people also are vital to our healing process. A Catch 22, really: Other people are important to our health, but not everyone is going to be healthy for us. Strangers who cannot or will not make a distinction between Alcoholism and alcohol abuse can be intentionally or unintentionally cruel. Friends, family and even helping professionals can be unintentionally unsupportive when they do not understand the disease, its consequences, and its course (including relapse). You can be shamed for having the disease, for not addressing it for as long as you did, and some people will even shame you for getting help . . . another thing that's not normal in our times. The stigma still tacked onto Alcoholism makes shame the minimum wage of sobriety: Some people get more, but we all get at least the minimum.

"Suck it up, you've been sober two years now, it's behind you." "It's NO disease." "How could you lapse? You're smarter than this." "Don't you have willpower?" I've heard all these uninformed comments. They all feel like someone grabbed a scab and started pulling. I was actually told once that I couldn't have felt any pain when I was drinking because I was drinking so much. That only demonstrated how a non-Alcoholic will never understand how an Alcoholic just does not feel a bombed, feeling-no-pain sensation from alcohol the way the normal people do. Normal people drink for fun. It isn't fun for us.

It is theorized that shame is the very reason Alcoholics and non-Alcoholics alike put alcohol into the body to begin with, dating way back to our *first* drink. Merle Fossum and Marilyn Mason, in *Facing Shame*, (W.W. Norton & Co., New York 1989) emphasize that if Alcoholics want to avoid taking their *next* drink, we must address shame.

Shame becomes a stressor when people we turn to, the institutions and caregivers we seek when we're recovering emotionally, physically, financially and legally dismiss us and discount our humanness, our experience and our disease. They see no difference between Alcohol Use Disorders.

Some sharks look a good deal like porpoises at first glance. Not upon close inspection though. Some people don't bother with the inspection and instead yell, "SHARK!" at the sign of a dorsal fin creasing the water. The thinking goes: It is convenient to loathe alcohol abusers, but there are some similar features to the Alcoholic that are difficult to discern without getting too close, so they're all the same. "SHARK!"

But I'm a porpoise.

I worked with counselors to create a simple chart to differentiate between Alcoholism and alcohol abuse, side by side, on a single page. The chart, which is APPENDIX II summarizes what most of society fails to acknowledge despite personal experience or professional training: There's an overlap, but there *is* a distinction between having the disease and being a garden-variety drunk.
The distinction between the two isn't always obvious, but the chart in APPENDIX II shows clear differences. The biggest is that alcohol abusers can quit but don't. "At a certain point in the drinking of every Alcoholic he passes into a state where the most powerful desire to stop drinking is of absolutely no avail." (From *Alcoholics Anonymous*) The point, though, is that most don't bother looking for a distinction. That's like not seeing a difference between the stomach flu and stomach cancer just because they both have similar signs.

When someone has the stomach flu, it is bad, but temporary. Like alcohol abuse. When someone has stomach cancer, it's bad, too, but it is a body change. Like Alcoholism. At times flu sufferers and cancer patients may feel the same pain but they aren't suffering the same condition. Same goes for the two Alcohol Use Disorders. What's more is that alcohol abusers actually *choose* the pain. The majority of the population doesn't get that.

People disbelieve Alcoholics in general. We lied sometimes to get our drink when we were practicing our craft. If AA taught me one thing it's that we Alcoholics are all horrible in the lie department. "I swear I only had two beers," doesn't even crack the top 20 of our lies. Of the handful of flaws shared by most of us, the one shared by every Alcoholic is a problem with honesty. For that we are distrusted for awhile or sometimes forever even after we stop drinking. Every lie took a toll, even the ones we told ourselves. The price tag, what it cost us, is our credibility. As a result, we're often not believed when we say we're struggling with a stressor or a trigger. This is a retaliatory brand of shame.

Other shamers will downplay the stressors if they believe us, possibly because the Symptoms of Sobriety do not make any sense to the 93 percent of the population that doesn't have the disease and its corresponding cortisol problem. The magnitude of the impact of the disease on *our* lives is beyond *their* experience, so we must be whining or exaggerating or simply have nothing to whine about because after all, they have stress, too. Some other shamers are people who just have genuine difficulty comprehending or being patient with the concept that you have been injured . . . or injured enough.

An even larger dose of shame comes when our character—not our genetics or our tissues—is what the shamers find faulty. They do not know Alcoholism is not an issue of character. Insisting there is a social or character explanation for a severe illness is so Paleolithic, so oddball, we really should be on *them* for such immature thinking. You become a scapegoat in their fantasy that bad things happen only to bad people. They believe they can shame you out of the disease. To them, willpower should have been enough like it is for those without the Alcoholic's genetic flaws and because you hadn't possessed enough willpower, your character is in question. You didn't want it bad enough. You're weak. You're sub-human. You're not normal.

The whopper of all shames can be summed up with a single word: Stigma. There is scorn toward the person, not the disease. There's ridicule of your struggle to move past the disease because it seems like such an easy thing to do to those who aren't Alcoholic. There are dime-store doctors diagnosing you as morally bankrupt, mentally weak or psychologically troubled. There's an implication that you're crying wolf for attention. There's a denial of services and access to life's pleasures and advancement opportunities that are ordinarily offered to more "normal" people. When people look at an Alcoholic all they see is a reflection of their beliefs on Alcoholism. Their opinions block their view of you as a man or woman. That's stigma.

There is direct punishment, taking away your rights in criminal or family courts if you have the unfortunate opportunity to be in them. The way the disease is misunderstood in the legal system is a tragic blunder of bureaucracy, but it is the nature of our antiquated retributive model of justice. Let me give you an example. I was told by a state employee that I "needed to be confined in order to focus on my alcohol addiction issues because it appears the alcohol problem led to broken relationships." No shit. But how about confining me because I drove while intoxicated, a law violation, not for getting two divorces in three years? She submitted that to a judge! Her assumption was spot on because two women left me over my drinking. But to recommend locking me up for my lapse because it led to broken relationships served to shame me for who I was years prior to my lapse, not for what I did the day I lapsed and got behind the wheel. Fortunately the judge ignored the subjective stigma of the employee's writing, but once I was out of the court and into the hands of corrections, her spurious opinion was treated as gospel and I was a bad person again, not a person who had done something bad. Lack of knowledge (or delicacy) on her part had legal consequence for me, not her. There would be no clinical assessment, I had already been assessed under the stigma Alcoholism carries. A couple months later, one of her colleagues, *a social worker leading a "treatment" program*, made a snarky comment that those of us arrested for OWI "were all raised in taverns." A vicious judgment of character and an insult to my mom who never once took me to a bar. Is that therapy? Or stigma?

That's just one example of stigma or ignorance leading to the insensitivity behind shame other people bring to our doorsteps or the shame we find when we stand on their doorsteps. In a lot of ways the shame is as pain-provoking as the disease itself, especially when we're treated this way by People Who Should Know Better. I once thought I had a huge fund of tolerance for people but realized it could be quickly drained once I began dealing with otherwise smart people who say dumb things about Alcoholism. The shamer may not want me to live in heaven because I've got this thing, but *I want to go anyway*, so who's the one with the problem? The Person Who Should Know Better. You do not expect them to build a shrine to your sobriety, but it isn't too much to expect them to let you try to succeed. They are simply not strong enough to accept that negative things can happen in life randomly. It is a part of nature they have chosen to deny. They have a "conflict of visions of reality" to steal from *Zen and the Art of Motorcycle Maintenance*. (Robert M. Pirsig, HarperCollins, New York 1974) It's the way people choose to see the world regardless of scientific discoveries.

Stigma is the shadow cast by ignorance, and ignorance about Alcoholism remains very strong in society. A poll cited in HBO's 2007 series, *Addiction: Why Can't They Just Quit?* reported that one half of the public believes Alcoholism is a "personal weakness." In the face of 50 years passing since the American Medical Association deemed Alcoholism a disease, half the population refuses to believe it is one and are wed to a 3000-year-old notion that it is a bad person rather than a bad medical condition. Call it lack of training or education to be more diplomatic, but it isn't going to change by the time you finish this book. According to a truly common way of thinking called the "just world philosophy," you've gotten what you deserved. In a just world, if you are careful, smart and moral you can avoid misfortune; and if you don't avoid misfortune, you *are* misfortune. Shame on you.

In 1957 Dr. Jellinek's disease model of Alcoholism authoritatively ended centuries of false conclusions about Alcoholism being tied to careful, smart and moral. People still have a hard time giving up the idea that it is some sort of problem like alcohol abuse that can be stopped by just walking in a different direction. They don't isolate the science from the myth and rhetoric. "Most people want to feel that issues are simple rather than complex," wrote J.A.C. Brown. (*Techniques of Persuasion*, Penguin Ballantine, New York 1963) "They want to have their prejudices confirmed, want to feel that they 'belong' with the implication that others do not, and need to pinpoint an enemy to blame for their frustrations." Such a philosophy is a form of imprecise thinking, about which Francis Bacon identified four broad types: Errors in thinking that are common to most people; Errors in thinking due to some personal bias; Misunderstanding language or context; and, Unquestioned acceptance of ideas. Three hundred years separate Brown and Bacon but both suggest the prevalence of shaming is a natural human tendency to be subjective rather than objective and that the untrained and closed mind will follow the path of least resistance. Ergo, the entire culture shames the Alcoholic, so too must they.

You weren't prepared for the disease any more than someone is prepared to get MS or diabetes. Who could be? It is unexpected. But even more unexpected are the rejection, the attacks and the insensitivity you're facing from such imprecise thinking or ignorance. You're Not Normal is a cruel cloud over sobriety's silver lining. The cruelty of shame hurts and you're already sensitive due to the cortisol. Dr. Matsakis adds that the adrenal gland changes in Alcoholics "can make you exceptionally sensitive to and observant of others' responses. Thus, even subtle cues in behavior of others will affect you more than they would a person [non-Alcoholic] who isn't distressed."

She adds, "Even when your desire to retaliate [to being shamed] is entirely justified, as it often is, an aggressive response only confirms their belief that you are a nut case or otherwise undeserving of assistance." Just picture how the state employees I mentioned earlier would have responded if I told them they were full of crap. Who'd be the nut case?

The shaming or labeling is cruel whether or not it is intended or gratuitous. Guilt is cruelty, too. You're cruel to yourself. I felt disappointment in myself deeply and sharply. But it was self-inflicted, and I could let myself off the hook. Shame is more cruel because you're not off the hook until someone lets you off the hook. Once you are labeled it is very difficult to escape the label. It has a permanence and becomes a yardstick by which your future performance is measured. You're looked upon as something they'd scrape off a shoe after a dog show. I've learned you're looked upon that way regardless of your professional success or social achievement before or after drinking changed your life. In the groundbreaking book, *Shame: The Power of Caring*, (Schenkman Books, Rochester, VI 1992) Gershan Kaufman clarifies how toxic such an identity becomes when you internalize it. "In itself, shame is a normal emotion. It tells us our limits, lets us know we can and will make a mistake . . . once shame is transformed into an identity, it becomes dehumanizing." Once someone identifies you and labels you as being the problem rather than having one and you internalize that label, you're no longer you.

Labels aren't always bad. We need the identification they provide us because we need to belong. The only thing more "normal" and basic is self-preservation. We can appreciate labels such as "dad" or "Midwestern." When labels aren't so great and we internalize the negative of not being normal, we are shamed and we become flawed and defective as human beings. Nothing about you is ok. You feel cut off. Alone. Apart. You feel like failure. You think you have to apologize frequently (covered extensively in the next chapter). You become unsure of your own opinions and hesitate to express them. You stop standing up for your beliefs and needs. You doubt you. Because you are flawed. Sound familiar?

**It comes in waves, too.** The first wave may not take out the shoreline of your sobriety, but the lapping of the waves one after another from different shamers will.

Your brain is an echo chamber for the words You're Not Normal. They are amplified, too. You hear over and over that you're flawed even when the words aren't spoken directly to you. Staying sober helps reduce the echoes, but they stubbornly refuse to vanish. The longer they hang on, the more the Symptoms hang on.

One of the foremost authorities on the impact of toxic shame is John Bradshaw. (*Healing the Shame that Binds*, Health Communications, Deerfield Beach, FL 1988) Bradshaw makes a direct connection between shame and lapse because alcohol provides an escape from the feelings you get from the Symptoms and the labels. Labels that don't fit but others have tagged onto you leave you feeling wounded. You want to medicate the wound by having a drink. You're caught between the dog and the hydrant. The shame causes stress . . . the shamer causes stress . . . not conforming to your body's request for a shot or two causes stress . . . and knowing you've never in your life just had one or two causes stress. Knowing you'll easily spiral back downward into the bottom of the V chart shown in APPENDIX I causes stress.

If/When you drink because of the shame someone else heaps onto you for being Alcoholic, the more right the shamer becomes. You prove their points. And you earn more shame. Bradshaw sees this cycle of shame begetting more shame and guilt as a squirrel cage, beginning at the point at which you've been labeled. You then want relief, you take a drink, get relief, then get shamed for getting the relief which puts you back to wanting relief from yet more shame.

Squirrel Cage

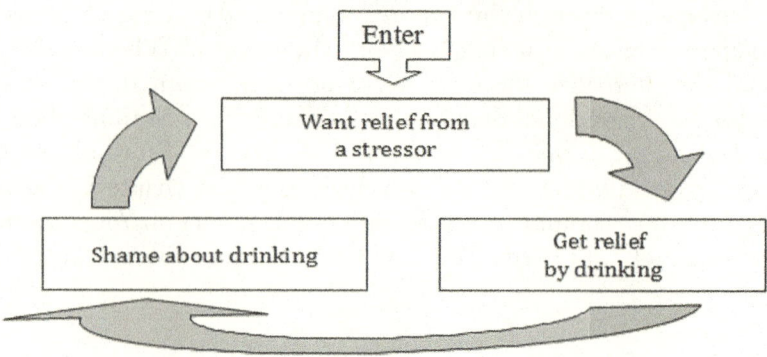

For an Alcoholic in sobriety, only a single spin through the squirrel cage—maybe two—and you're well on the path from lapse to relapse.

People expect more out of someone who's put his Alcoholism into remission. There's the expectation that the Alcoholic avoids relapse. Forever. There's the demand that he achieves new levels of productivity on the job. He's not allowed other human problems, like overeating. They insist he pursues spiritual enlightenment. And if he fails in any of these areas, they're actually disappointed in him and label him again as a failure—as if non-Alcoholics routinely achieve such goals. Just because you never can drink does not mean you never can be allowed to live without someone reminding you of it each day.

You don't need to have a really low bottom to have attracted shamers. People shame high-bottom Alcoholics, too, whether or not they've been a victim of his drinking. These are the people who are on you for having a disease like ants are on a popsicle melting on the sidewalk. There will always be some Bozo who is going to help you into the squirrel cage because shamers and shame go hand-in-hand with Alcoholism. The three most common sources from which shame originates are the family, schools and community/culture.

Shames from the family system develop from passed-down patterns, similar to how we learn to guilt ourselves. Shamers get it from their parents who got it from theirs. Sigmund Freud and Carl Jung wrote brilliantly on the shame learned from the family system that results from fear of physical and emotional abandonment. Aren't we all loved for our compliance with our family's way of thinking? If the household believes Alcoholics are trash, the offspring is likely to glom onto that way of thinking. So the family packs this shaming lunch for the kid and he or she is trotted off to school—shame source two. The school systems reinforce this idea of normal and a new concept of perfectionism. The shamer gets an idea that 100 percent is the magic number and no other grade will do, and this gets pasted onto the idea that Alcoholics are less than 100 percent. Never mind that normal a.k.a. average is 80 and passing is 70-something, the Alcoholic is a failure. Here's where some of life's most lasting judgments are cemented because other kids validated what we learned at home about Alcoholics and we learned the idea that success was a matter of applying yourself.

This should be enough training ground for the people who put enormous pressure on those struggling with sobriety. Their ideas are then firmed up in religion, culture and community as adults. Judeo-Christian teaching starts it off with the teaching that we're all bad from the womb. God will forgive, but where it gets sloppy is that He isn't judging you, the people in the church on the corner are. You're judged for what you did, not who you are. What started as a "bad" from the shamer's education at home, is now a "sin." Culture and community are no less shaming because the word "sin" is swapped out for the term "community values" and Alcoholism is an undesirable one.

According to the "Faces of Recovery" survey in 2001, four in ten people in sobriety said they experienced shame and social embarrassment as a result of these three sources of shame. Shamers label you as a pariah. The label is one, giant, cortisol-laced stressor. It becomes emotionally and physically uncomfortable for us to protect ourselves from the labels and stigma. Alcoholism is "bad," it isn't "perfect," it's a "sin" and it doesn't conform to "community values." You're Not Normal. This place called Not Normal . . . It's a lonely place to be.

You internalize the label and feel sorry for yourself and start to drink over the loneliness and you hop into the squirrel cage. There is no soft landing out of it either.

You're Not Normal causes too much damage and that is power we're giving the shamer. I let it get to me, like most Alcoholics do, and giving someone the power to make me feel miserable created intolerable damage when I chose to drink over it. The damage was the loss of my sobriety, sure, but the resulting fallout was far worse. I cried plenty of silent tears over the skinned knees of my children when I wasn't there to comfort them because I was in treatment or jail because of relapse. On Christmas Eve I wasn't there to eat cookies on Santa's behalf when the kids left them out before bedtime in anticipation of his visit. I was devastated not to give the hugs my children needed but didn't get. You know the moments when their little chins begin to quiver because they don't know if they can or should cry but want to and they are searching for dad to know it is ok? I missed those moments. I lost seeing the sparklers reflected in their eyes on Independence Day. There were drawings I didn't collect from their backpacks after school but had to retrace with my own hands when I opened my mail in jail. The kids were damaged by my shoddy handling of shame and look at what I missed, too. I broke their hearts and my own. I can feel guilt over those things. Who has the right to shame me over that and to tell me I am a bad dad for missing the skinned knees and Christmas cookies? Who is the authority on whether or not I am entitled to the tears I shed? We're all capable of accepting consequences for our actions. But it isn't up to the shamers to put us in our places over our shortcomings as dads because the shamers have some backward idea about how we lack willpower or morals. We fail when we give them that kind of power. Shame is a knife that way. The extent of injury has nothing to do with the toughness of your skin, only the sharpness of the blade and the force of the person behind it.

==There is no bigger barrier to recovery than giving someone the power to shame us. The right to be the final judge of yourself is what you strip from yourself by internalizing shame. When you drink over how someone else judges you, you've only proven them right.==

Can you forgive them for judging you? Not forgiving costs you as much or more than it costs the other guy.

Chapter Six

"We read that we ought to forgive our enemies; but we do not read that we ought to forgive our friends."—Cosimo DeMedici

Evil, inadequately informed and incompetent people DO exist. A person is not automatically one of them just because he has Alcoholism, but given the chance your friends and neighbors automatically label you that way when you have the disease. Such emotional labeling can lead directly into a minefield of apologies and forgiveness.

Like any emotionally loaded situations, the disease and struggling with sobriety are springboards to what could be open and honest apologies and healthy amendsmaking. Amends are part of wrestling our humility back from the booze. The act of forgiveness—seeking it or giving it—however, is an enormous stressor. Relax though, it's a hard experience for people without drinking problems, too. You might say it's "normal" to struggle with forgiveness. Enduring the shaming and blaming—justified or unjustified, informed or uninformed—brings you to the process of forgiveness and three common scenarios which elevate cortisol . . .

When *you* seek forgiveness,
When others insist you seek theirs, and
When you are the forgiver.

Each may seem really touchy-feely but represent hard work that pressures the adrenal system into releasing cortisol and triggering the Symptoms of Sobriety.

When an Alcoholic seeks forgiveness

Forgiveness has been romanticized for its powerful effect on wellbeing. But as seductive as getting well and being forgiven are, forgiveness isn't all that simple to seek.

While under the influence of the disease, we do wrong. A lot of wrongs. Mind you not everything was wrong, but our brilliant judgment was impaired, and we did some really inexcusable things while impaired. Alcohol works that way on normal people, too. It loosens lips or inhibitions, or both, even in the man or woman with the most sophistication and integrity or the highest standards. That's no justification, just a fact, demonstrated at any black tie affair as abundantly as at bar time at the local meat-market bar. It's also fact that alcohol-fueled interactions leave one or both sides feeling a need to seek forgiveness or a need to say, "I'm sorry."

One of the greatest reminders of how complicated we tend to make things is right in Robert Fulghum's *All I Really Need to Know I Learned in Kindergarten.* (Ballantine Books, New York 2004) It is among his basics: "Saying you're sorry when you hurt somebody." That's the lesson practiced by every Alcoholic at some point in their sobriety. It's the low-hanging fruit every Alcoholic, even if they don't hang around 12-step groups long enough to make amends in the ninth step. Saying "I'm sorry" is a good start but it only nicks the surface of seeking forgiveness.

You can't seek forgiveness methodically the way you look for a lost sock or a book at Barnes and Noble or toothpaste in the grocery store. Fulghum's right, apology is that easy . . . but forgiveness is far from being that easy. Forgiveness isn't organized. It's a volatile mix of timing and personality and one critical ingredient: Forgiving yourself. Phychologists call it self-compassion. When an Alcoholic hasn't started overcoming guilt and forgiven himself for stuff that was actually said or done, he cannot go looking for forgiveness from others.

Not forgiving yourself is a sin of pride known as scrupulousity. Not sin as in biblical, capital-S Sin but a sin as in an infraction against your own well-being. The term grows out of the same Latin root as scruples from a preceding chapter and was popularized in the 1960s in several psychologists' writings, especially that of O. Hobart Mowrer. (*A New Group Therapy*, Insight Books, Princeton, NJ 1964) By the way, when Alcoholics are jailed, this forgiveness-of-self process is stunted, increasing the probability of relapse upon release because self-forgiveness does not happen in that environment. "The experience undermines self-forgiveness on a daily basis," says Casarjian. "Interaction after interaction fosters shame and reinforces the self-concept of the [Alcoholic] as an inferior person who has not been forgiven and never will be."

Self-forgiveness is not redefining an offense as a non-offense, or condoning behavior that is hurtful/insensitive/abusive/lacking in maturity. It's not excusing or overlooking actions or absolving yourself of responsibility. It's simply not resenting yourself for your actions or your illness.

So if you expect to be forgiven, you are compelled to forgive. Forgiveness and unforgiveness cross pollinate each other. Think about it this way: If *you* can't forgive you, you can't realistically expect others to forgive you. If you expect someone to forgive you first in order to forgive yourself, you may be in for a heck of a wait.

When you forgive you, you're on your way but still have to contend with those other volatile ingredients of timing and personality. You're on your own with timing. The-sooner-the-better vs. time-heals-all-wounds. From my own experience, time never healed a thing, but my cynicism shouldn't color your decisions. Trust your instincts for once. You are entitled to do that again. Personality is a potential barrier to getting the forgiveness you seek regardless of timing because bitterness trumps timing every time.

Forgiveness is social health. In sobriety, we're required to pay a lot of attention to physical health and mental health, as a result social health gets shoved down the list of priorities. That can make some people bitter about forgiving you because it can appear that you have complete apathy about the damage you have done. There's an arbitrary "full" line on the container that holds how much of your crap someone will take and in the eyes of some people you have passed the full line long ago while you were still drinking and now they've got to watch you focus on *your* physical and mental needs? (Not to create more guilt for you . . . but it is your fault for breaching that full line, not theirs for having one.)

How you identify bitterness is quite simple. Bitterness remembers details. Humans have millions of conversations and interactions in a lifetime, most long forgotten. When someone remembers every statement word for word, every detail play by play, it is bitterness. It isn't just a stellar memory. People do not mull over such detail of good things this way. Only the bad things get burned into memory with such detail. This way the bitter can focus on precisely how right they are and how wrong the Alcoholic was/is. And how much of an apology is due.

When an Alcoholic doesn't hold up well to this bitterness—sometimes hostility—or when seeking forgiveness, cortisol increases because of that fight-or-flight instinct. It is a threatening situation.

Both sides need the social health created by forgiveness. Even the bitter person. Whether he comprehends that or not. There is a physical health benefit for both sides, too, discovered by the Menninger Clinic in the 1970s. Forgiveness, getting it or giving it, creates improvement in your psychological health and physical health follows. It's called the Psychophysiological Principle. (Elmer Green and Dale Walters, "Voluntary Control of Internal States: Psychological and Physiological," in *Journal of Transpersonal Psychology*, 1970) Green and Walters prove every change in the psychological state is accompanied by an appropriate change in the physiological state and is conversely true." A fancy way of saying your mind improves your body and vice versa. That's cortisol, actually. An identical conclusion on the physical health differences beween those who forgive and those who don't was done in the 1990s by Charlotte van Oyen Witvliet at Hope College, so it is worth your time and health and worth the health of those you've offended or injured to make things good.

How much do you persevere? Honestly, you have to cut your losses with a bitter person at some point. The Jewish tradition may have it right and may save you from obsessing over forgiveness. Their tradition has been around for three millennia at any rate. Jews ask three times for forgiveness, and if it is still refused, you have done all you can and the burden (and the cortisol problem) shifts to the other party. I grew up Catholic . . . so that tradition translates into trying 16 times and then guilting yourself for the rest of your life. I'll go with the Jews on this one. Accept that no matter how contrite you are for stuff you actually did, some people will continue to refuse your apology because some people still think you are the problem, not the alcohol.

"Without forgiveness, life is governed by an endless cycle of resentment and retaliation," according to Roberto Assaglioli. (*Psychosynthesis*, Penguin Books, New York 1979) Avoid that cycle by holding up your end of the bargain and trying to seek forgiveness. Four centuries before Jesus led a bunch of fishermen into one of the world's largest movements of spirituality and forgiveness lived a Greek known as Democritis. He was one of the first philosophers, living around the time of Socrates and his student Plato but developing ideas that have lived longer in application than the ideas of either of the more famous

Greeks of his era. Democritis said, "Repentance for wrong doing is the saving grace of life." That's wrong doing, not wrong being. The idea that you are wrong because you did wrong or because you have a disease is nothing for which to repent or seek forgiveness: Their lack of knowledge about Alcoholism is their problem. Don't make resentment yours.

It could be worse. For 300 years, lack of knowledge about epilepsy led to hundreds of epileptics being judged as witches and burned at the stake. Polissena of San Macario is one famous example. People like her were treated with wrath over having a disease no one understood. With Alcoholics in our century, the wrath looks like withholding forgiveness—or demanding that you ask for it.

When others insist an Alcoholic seeks their forgiveness

The fantasy is that some people who demand an apology from an Alcoholic is that it "creates closure." The reality is that it creates resentment, a cortisol-heavy burden. Regardless of how sincerely you are in apologizing to people who think they're owed one, your words will never be enough.

Leo Buscaglia, an icon of pop psychology in the 1980s known as Dr. Hug, harshly critiques people who demand an apology as vengeful. "Forgiveness can never be realized in an atmosphere of accusation, condemnation and fault-finding." (*Loving Each Other*, Fawcett Columbine, New York 1984) When you get pulled into someone's you-have-to-apologize-to-me fault-finding drama, you permit yourself to be devalued. A disease is not a sufficient reason to devalue a human no matter how poorly you acted while drinking.

You can also view the demand as their creating an opportunity to forgive you. That one-upmanship is still a condemnation of you and when they do forgive after granting you an opportunity to apologize, their words are empty. They do not absolve. Instead it is their way of saying, "I judge you worthy of forgiveness and forgive you because I am morally superior. In my great benevolence your trespass is forgiven and for that you must be dutifully grateful." (David Augsburger, *The New Freedom of Forgiveness*, Moody Publishers, Chicago 2000) Forgiveness is a transaction and they are not participating, they're grandstanding.

They will never be happy with your apology no matter how heartfelt. The elephant in the room: You are never on the hook for the happiness of someone else. In the 12-step world, a premium is placed on apologizing to those we've harmed. It's step nine. We're not apologizing to make them happy, we're apologizing to save our own happiness.

The steps are in order for a good reason: Step four gives us a list of concrete and demonstrable things we've done wrong so by the time we hit step nine we know why we're saying I'm sorry. Just because someone isn't happy with us won't make the inventory in step four. It is too subjective and isn't concrete enough to jeopardize your sobriety. The process of recovery leans heavily upon compassion and forgiveness but the therapeautic value only applies to the concrete hurts, not solving happiness for other people. As much as we might wish good things for one another, we don't have the ability to create happiness for someone who's unhappy with us for carrying a disease. You can only please someone like that temporarily by giving them the opportunity to pardon you. That's miles from making amends, miles from forgiveness and miles from compassion. It's manipulation and shaming.

When someone mistakes the disease for a voluntary and intentional behavior or imagines it to be something you chose, the manner in which they'll fish for an apology could sound like: "You missed a lot while you were in rehab." Open-ended and loaded with shame. A litmus test for detecting true complaints and separating them from the fishing is this: If there is a solution to the woe allegedly caused by you having a disease, are you personally responsible for that solution? The solution we all need to focus on is staying sober, and we'll fail at it if we keep ratcheting up our cortisol by chasing after someone's need to put themselves above us. Of all the characters who march across the stage of your recovery, misinformed manipulators are the most potentially harmful.

A manipulator demanding an apology is almost without fail a person who has a belief system that tells them the logical explanation for Alcoholism is that it is a choice. As a result their injury is that they feel you chose the disease. There are millions of sometimes goofy bits of misinformation that find their way from comforting thoughts to becoming "logical explanations." If you get cancer, you ate too much red meat. If your husband left, you drove him to it. If an infant dies, it was God's will. If you get Alcoholism, you chose to get Alcoholism. Faulty belief systems aren't your hang-ups to solve. Logic is what other people try to use to prove you are wrong. Their logic is not logical.

Alcoholism isn't. Period.

A lethal disease that kills with an undeniable need to consume a toxic substance yet will still kill you when you deny it the toxic substance is not logical. You can see how that *won't* be logical to most people, however, because non-Alcoholics have no idea how it feels to *have to* drink. Nine out of 10 people who are not in the counseling or medical professions still have belief systems that Alcoholism is a disease of willpower. To them it is far from logical to think it is a biochemical problem, not a moral one. I'm fond of pointing out that mice don't even like the smell or flavor or alcohol. It repels them actually. They don't have morals, either. So how do scientists gather up alcoholic mice for alcohol research if Alcoholism is a moral problem? They breed them. The Alcoholic mice are Not Normal. The genes are tweaked. The mouse morals aren't tweaked, and the alcohol is not altered to trick them into tasting it. They are bred with a biological condition, not a psychological condition. Dr. James Milian and Katherine Ketcham point out, "Psychological factors play no stronger role in Alcoholism than they play in causing any other chronic illness." (*Under the Influence*, Madrona Publishers, Seattle, WA 1981) And that is a leap of logic many people are unwilling to take. Despite the weight of medical evidence, there will be those in the path of your recovery who have a belief system which simply will not permit them to accept a biological explanation. It's something you did and they want an apology.

Demand for an apology is a trap. When you apologize, you do not correct their flawed belief system, you confirm it and it is used as a basis for judging you and your next moves. Statistically, an Alcoholic is likely to lapse, so you're also likely to have the apology trap sprung on you more than once. Then it sounds something like: "You were doing so well. Why lapse?" Like we chose the misery. Like we chose to feel the Symptoms of Sobriety.

In Chapter Eight several solutions are suggested as a way to ease or prevent the Symptoms brought out by stressors like forgiveness, but I'll tee up one suggestion here as it specifically pertains to people who think they're owed a chance to forgive you. Instead of capitulating with an undeserved apology, try this: "You're right. That was a dumb thing I went through." Ten words. None of them was an apology nor an attempt to correct a faulty belief system. You told him he is right. Who doesn't like hearing that? And you admitted your humanness. Nothing else. The manipulator gave himself permission to demand an apology based on his beliefs, these 10 words give you permission to take the demand off the table. Forgiveness, after all, is a right of the injured, not the naïve.

Resist the temptation to correct the belief system or to turn the tables on him. Here's why telling him he is right makes sense. There are 21 million Americans with the disease. That means about 287 million have no idea how it feels to have to drink. They don't get what it is like to drink Alcoholically and cannot or will not accept anything but an outdated concept of Alcoholism as a psychological or moral failure. The numbers are against us. Try the 10 words with any of them that get in your business fishing for an apology. You'll be surprised how liberating it is from the Symptoms.

The 10-word statement is an example of fogging, which is deflecting shame by acknowledging a truth while still allowing *you* to be the judge of your actions. Fogging came out of the Behavior Therapy heyday of the '60s in Southern California. Emotional sensitivity is a common Symptom. That's why we so often feel compelled to give in to shame or demands for apology. A technique like fogging helps desensitize ourselves. Fogging blocks off—like a fog bank would—those who believe you chose Alcoholism. Fogging also helps resolve the cortisol-inducing internal conflict you feel between what you know about the disease and what you wish other people knew. Fogging is also called, "Negative Assertiveness" by psychologists. It works to stave off guilt, shamers, apology seekers and generally any thinking that Alcoholism is an abomination or atrocity. I have more on assertiveness a couple chapters ahead.

Let me reinforce something from earlier in this chapter though: Be responsible. If you did wrong and really hurt someone, be honest with yourself about it. This section of the chapter only deals with those who are forcing contrition out of you just because you're Alcoholic. Apologize for your bad behavior, not your bad genes.

There is a misperception behind this stressor that you have to have the forgiveness of other people in order to deal with them more effectively . . . that forgiveness keeps the peace or greases the sticky wheels of social interactions . . . something like that. "I'm sorry," is powerful that way, yet it simply is not an effective way of dealing with manipulators. Giving in to them is like feeding a stray cat. They'll keep coming around. Once you give in to someone who shames you into an apology, you've fed their myth that an Alcoholic is Not Normal because of the disease. They'll keep coming back seeking additional apologies and more atonement the way the stray believes the food dish will be set out. No matter how hangdog you look or sincere you sound, you'll never be sorry enough, just like you'll never shake that stray. At some point, you have to stop setting out the dish. Fogging works for that.

You do risk losing that person. If they're genuine and open-minded (two things you need from other people) they'll come around again once they realize the payoff they were seeking isn't going to come. So what if it gets chilly for awhile.

There aren't style points awarded for making it through sobriety with a huge flock of followers. *Your* recovery is on the line, not theirs. You're not on the hook for their happiness and you cannot live in terror of hurting someone's feelings by not giving in to a naïve and manipulative demand for apology.

Why people use forgiveness as manipulation tool this way with an Alcoholic was observed by psychologist Manuel Smith's clinical research. (*When I Say No I Feel Guilty*, Bantam Books, New York 1975) He postulates that manipulators have a hidden anxiety agenda and have no proper way of dealing with their own neurosis so they take it out on you. For example, they fear being left alone if alcohol kills you or they fear financial fallout if you go back to rehab or they fear public embarrassment if they're spotted with you. Those are their neuorses, not yours. "Manipulators are not always cruel bastards or bitches with malignant intent, but mostly anxious, insecure people who are coping the way they know how: Manipulating others to make *them* feel anxious and shamed," Smith wrote.

Regardless of motivation or neuroses the manipulator is a tremendous obstacle for your intention to recover. Try as you may in sobriety, you can't run from your own shadow. (Sometimes, the clichés get it right.) In the eyes of some people you'll always be seen in your Alcoholic role, the one you played during your worst drinking. It's sort of like Christopher Knight always being seen in his pre-teen role as Peter Brady on the '70's sitcom *The Brady Bunch* and Leonard Nimoy always Spock from *Star Trek*. What if the only role by which we knew Clint Eastwood was Rowdy Yates of *Rawhide*? What other roles and Oscars would we ignore blindly? You don't need your shadow or the role from you crummiest days of drinking to be the reason people seek the right to grant you forgiveness. You may have to be the one forgiving them for their neuroses or naivete.

When you are the forgiver

When you get wrapped up in how others have injured you with manipulation or shaming it is just as physically unhealthy as feeling unforgiven as the studies earlier in this chapter pointed out. So a healthy recovery is going to rely upon you forgiving other people, too. We Alcoholics really suck at this. We grip resentments like a chubby trick-or-treater grips a bag full of Snickers. We have to—*have to*—knock that off and forgive, even the people who are downright hostile toward us.

You will be able to initiate the process with someone by whom you feel hurt in about two-thirds of the situations. Most of your injurers are not going to come knocking on your door seeking a clean slate for judging you, and the other third are likely to have slammed the door on you and moved on from your drama. Remember the "full" line you passed.

==Forgiveness isn't a pardon==, releasing a person from accountability for the injury they caused. Pardon, a la President Ford pardoning Nixon, assumes one person has authority over another.

==Forgiveness isn't forgetting either.== Author Beverly Flannigan (*Forgiving the Unforgiveable*, Macmillan Publishing, New York 1992) says you have to remember to forgive someone. "To forgive, one must remember the past, put it into perspective and move beyond it. Without rememberance, no wound can be transcended."

To transcend or close wounds with the two thirds who haven't slammed the door to you, ==forgiveness is a transaction.== The Transactional Model follows a sequence described in 1953 by J.A. Martin ("A Realistic Theory of Forgiveness," in *The Return to Reason*, Henry Regnery Press, Chicago).

A) Injured accused injurer
B) Injurer admits it
C) Injured gives reasons he feels violated
D) Injurer admits he was wrong
E) Injured punishes
F) Injurer takes it
G) Injured seeks assurance it won't happen again
H) Injurer promises
I) Injured accepts the promise and requires nothing further
J) Injurer trusts forgiveness is permanent

That's pretty civilized, optimistic and tidy. And it works. You've probably practiced the model without the extensive analysis since you played in a sandbox. But the model is hardly realistic when you encounter the kind of bitterness Alcoholics face. The emotional sensitivity doesn't help and creates an imbalance in the model because the belief systems of injurer and injured are out of whack. Steps C and D can become a snarl when one side doesn't accept the difference between drinking problems and problem drinkers. If the bitterness persists, you may have to walk away with the satisfaction that you tried: You attempted the transaction.

There's hope still, even when the Transactional Model fails or is inappropriate because someone slammed the door on you and is long gone, unable to participate in the transaction. They're gone believing *they* have been injured. Without the opportunity to confront the injurer, you're pretty much left to repair the damage and wipe the slate clean by yourself. This solo battle is conflict. Conflict drives cortisol. The hope for this conflict is the Solitary Model of forgiveness.

Flannigan's Solitary Model has been used successfully in overcoming unresolved conflict when a victim cannot face an injurer because the injurer is gone, dead or unwilling to find fault with his own belief system (Step D in the Transactional Model). She explains that three injuries happen when someone walks away from us the way one of three in an Alcoholics social circle inevitably do by the time we stop drinking.

These *are* injuries. Even if not intentional toward you—if someone is just walking away from your drama—there's still harm. The injury can be long-lasting and you will continue to feel the Symptoms without an initiative to forgive the injurer *without him around*. Flannigan calls it "Mastery over your wound." "It's the process through which an injured person fights off, then embraces, then conquers a situation on his or her own."

Just because someone else isn't involved doesn't mean solitary forgiveness comes about in a quiet or passionless way. Mine was as noisy as kindergarten playgrounds. That's because it's an investment of re-examining you own assumptions about other people and that's no small, tranquil task since you've likely held these assumptions a long time.

You're not going to feel balanced in sobriety until you feel the scales are balanced with those you feel injured you. The six phases of Flannigan's Solitary Model are:

    A) Name the injury
    B) Claim it
    C) Blame the injurer
    D) Balance the scales
    E) Choose to forgive
    F) Move on

You can see some overlap with the older, two-sided Transactional Model and it's important in either model to know upon whose rules on terms of "right" and "wrong" are being relied as the yardstick of whether or not an injury happened. That's the crux of this chapter and the previous one on shame: Did you both understand the disease the same way?

When you're in the Solitary Model, you're naming the injury (Step A) based upon *your* understanding of the disease and that an Alcoholic would not choose Alcoholism, wouldn't choose its progression or its course and wouldn't choose its duration. It's about chromosomes and tissues and ethanol molecules, not willpower, and you can have a right to feel injured by anyone who refuses the scientific evidence.

The second phase of the Solitary Model is to detangle all the other related injuries. You're not entitled to be defensive about stuff you really did, but you can be defensive about others misunderstanding you. Blame the injurer for that (Step C) and not yourself any longer. Realize the most important word in this paragraph is "misunderstanding" as in their belief system, their neuroses or naivete. Their belief system, their understanding, was based upon bad information. It may seem like you're caving in, but the most efficient way to forgive someone who walked away from the forgiveness transaction is to accept you know more about the disease than they do and your choice to recover, on the scales, is way heavier than their ignorance.

There are some who will spend a lifetime driving up their own cortisol because they want so badly to balance the scales with someone who walked away. It becomes an obsession if you don't walk away, too.

Forgiveness is final. The past is over once you're forgiven and there's no longer any interpretation of who is more right or wrong. In interpreting the meaning of your injury and others' injuries (real or perceived) you've got to accept—as hokey as this sounds—that when you find forgiveness it does forever change your relationship. Roles change when you are Alcoholic. Dreams die. There are plenty of what-could-have-beens. You have to let go of them and old dreams and old roles. Not forgiving a person because we're afraid of grieving over the old relationship or old roles will poison you with cortisol. Which is why grief is the fourth of our stressors.

Chapter Seven

"The grief that does not speak
Whispers the o'er fraught heart,
And bids it to break."
—William Shakespeare, *Macbeth*, Act IV, Scene iii

You will not find recovery without the process of mourning. Most people will want to pull that off, but you can't. Period. There is no conceivable scenario to avoid mourning in sobriety. You cannot go from drinking to recovery by skipping the pain of grief any more than you can go directly from Kindergarten to college. "After all, if our life is altered so dramatically by our trauma that we can hardly recognize it as our own, we might think it as a death," says Kathryn Cramer. (*Staying on Top When Your World Turns Upside Down*, Penguin Books, New York 1990) "In a small but real way our life as we once knew it has died." Death and grief go hand in hand.

You have a grievable loss. Failure to grieve, failure to grieve appropriately (e.g. without booze), or failing to even identify our losses as losses, sacks more attempts at long-term recovery than any other stressor. One thing few people respect or even notice about Alcoholics is the upheaval and loss we go through. Instead people seem more interested in the upheaval and loss we create.

Attention in group therapy is showered on abstinence. But look to those who have the most experience in their own recoveries and you'll see people who have identified their losses, grieved them and transcended them. Every single one of them knows fully what he or she lost and is over it. Grief—the process, not the noun—belongs in treatment for Alcoholism. A full, real grief process. Not the infomercial version. It doesn't happen in a series of handouts or a couple of DVDs. There are no shortcuts, and because there aren't it is often overlooked in short-term treatment efforts. Mourning has to be an essential part of recovery's curriculum. The carnage Alcoholism causes in our lives needs to be seen in the same light as grief counselors view a loss such as a natural disaster or untimely death.

Grieving is a lengthy process that usually takes months, but often lasts years. Nobody is particularly good at it. Who wants to be? We could all stand a little coaching, which is one thing noticeably absent in programs focused only on compliance/abstinence. Part of an Alcoholic DIES when you remove alcohol. Those nine words *beg* for a period of mourning. Recovery is contingent upon it and learning to live with the loss. If the loss isn't mourned, it triggers more cortisol.

Losses, by the way, can have a cumulative effect. If you lost a pet while you were drinking, you probably medicated yourself with booze and never mourned. If you were in a car wreck, you probably didn't manage that loss effectively. Once you're sober, these things from the past may be lurking underneath the financial/social/professional/self-identity losses from the disease.

When you grieve, you express loss at three intertwined levels braided tightly together.

Grief's Braid

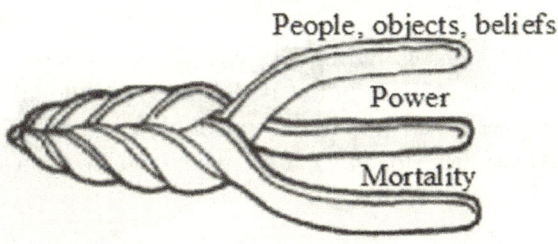

The primary strand in grief is the specific person, object or belief you have lost. For the chronic Alcoholic, this strand could be his health. You mourn the lost ideal of your health and vitality. Seemingly they are shattered and no longer exist, certainly not the way you once had them before Alcoholism's toll. Financial loss also goes in this strand. Marriages irretrievably broken go here. Mine weren't great, but that doesn't mean I wanted them to end. I had to mourn them since I drank right through the losses previously. Career loss goes here, too. That was a major one for me: I spent years training in a career I won't ever have again.

Also as part of the first strand you grieve over the people in the previous chapter you may have driven away from you. You mourn the people plus you mourn a belief you held that spouses, family and friends stood behind you when you're sick.

The loss an Alcoholic feels after a lapse goes along this first strand, too. Lapse can drive off additional people or people who were just coming back to your side, but lapse also kills a belief that everyone attempting sobriety shares: I've had my last drink. You lapse and you're bumping a really fresh wound.

You may have also lost trust, another belief or ideal. You trust the integrity of people or the legal or medical systems. If you cherished this philosophy of trust as I did, you had a rude eye opener once you tried to get help or started picking up your pieces. Losing this core philosophy brings about a sheer, lung-crushing grief over not being allowed to believe in others coupled with a feeling the You're Not Normal and not permitted back into the mainstream.

Here's the spot where the first strand touches closely the second strand, which involves your perception of power and your actual power. Your freedom, for example. Feeling booted out of the mainstream is as power-robbing as being arrested and locked up. No matter how talented or persuasive you are, no matter how impressively sincere you are you cannot totally reclaim your spot in the mainstream and roles or prestige or value you held. That's the stigma of Alcoholism.

The first of the 12 steps is "admitting you are powerless over alcohol." It may be a liberating statement, but it is definitely a saddening statement of loss. I have no power when it comes to alcohol. You cannot get that power back like non-Alcoholics do. No matter what you do, you cannot become non-Alcoholic.

The third strand, grieving the loss of your immortality, is wrapped closely to the other two strands. In fact, the realization that you could die from this disease is the ultimate acknowledgement of the second strand, loss of power, as well as the first strand, loss of health or beliefs. The awareness of the proximity of your own death is the fundamental reason why mourning *anything* (the death of a pet, the loss of a spouse, a severed limb, etc.) is so difficult. As I waited for a bed to open up in rehab in Chandler, Ariz., I read a newspaper story of a student at Arizona State University who died of alcohol poisoning. His BAC was .31. He was dead . . . how many times had I passed that BAC? I even doubled it. I was now really aware of the proximity of my own death.

Alcholism is fatal, not just for the overdosing, but more on that later. I had played with death and I'm never far from it with this disease. That's when the third strand hit home to me. I was no longer immortal.

The strands are traumas that affect stress and its cortisol response. The traumas or losses with the highest scores on the scale in Chapter Two involve change and/or mortality. We literally have to grieve if our social or mental health is to survive these strands, these losses. Barbara Snell Dohrenwend's "Classification and Rating of Stressful Life Events" (*Journal of Health and Social Behavior*, 1978) shows that Alcoholics who resist mourning resist *living* because all 10 of her most stressful events involve loss . . .

1) Child dies
2) Spouse dies
3) Illness diagnosis
4) Going to jail
5) Divorce
6) Birth of first child
7) Couldn't get a cure or treatment
8) Getting convicted of crime
9) Infertility
10) Staying in a bad relationship

. . . and many of these things are in our Alcoholic lives. The only variable seems to be the depth of the mournable loss from Alcoholic to Alcoholic, not whether or not we have something to mourn.

The depth of the grief and the litany of individual losses connected to the disease can seem impossibly huge. How can anyone process all that grief? How do you eat an elephant? One bite at a time. ==The first bite is permitting yourself to believe you have losses . . . the last bite is accepting the losses and living with them.==

==Acceptance== is a lengthy commitment to coping and getting healthier . . . two things at which we're notoriously bad. The key, is ==patience== (another thing noticeably absent on our list of virtues) because acceptance does not come overnight. You focus on the goal of taking that last bite, meanwhile taking a lot of little bites to keep your losses from interfering with the day-to-day stuff you do to maintain sobriety, like getting enough sleep. The first bite though is letting yourself believe you *have* losses. Allowing yourself to feel loss instead of struggling against admitting them expedites the whole process. It's like the

Chinese finger trap, an intricately woven child's toy that holds you firmer the more you struggle against it. You stop struggling, and you're free of the trap. Some experts refer to this part of the grief process as surrender or letting go. Another appropriate term would be validation.

You validate that you are hurt by your loss and you're no less entitled to feel loss than non-Alcoholics. If something was significant to you and it is lost or changed for the worse, mourning is appropriate and necessary despite how a shamer might claim you're not entitled to grief. The worst of the advice they give is to drop it and move on. Or as Executive Officer Kermit Tyler said, "Don't worry about it." More about Tyler later. When others don't advise you to validate your loss, it's usually that they're consumed with dwelling on their losses from your chaos. Your losses may be less tangible to them, but losses of your beliefs or status or health are still real. You need to respect them, validate them.

What comes after that first bite is a series of other bites or stages before you get to acceptance. Various views of the grief process break the stages down distinctly but there's a great deal of overlap. The Bradshaw book mentioned two chapters ago identifies the stages as:

Shock, Denial, Bargaining, Depression, Anger, Remorse, Sadness, Hurt, Loneliness, Acceptance.

Dr. Harold Bloomfield (*Making Peace With Your Past*, HarperCollins, New York 2000) condenses the stages into three groupings:

Shock/Denial, Anger/Fear/Sadness, Understanding/Acceptance

Ashley Davis Prend (*Transcending Loss*, Berkeley, New York 1997) also has three stages:

Shock, Disorganization, Reconstruction

Each of those renowned experts borrows from Elisabeth Kubler Ross' seminal work, the 1969 book *On Death and Dying*, (Macmillan, New York) which is considered by many psychologists to be the textbook on mourning. She presents five stages terminally ill persons may go through after learning of their terminal diagnosis. What she presented was a summary of what dying people use as coping mechanisms. Over the decades, healthcare workers, nurses, clergy, caregivers, professors and other readers of her book mutated the summary into the Five Stages of Grief.

Denial/Isolation, Anger/Resentment, Bargaining, Depression, Acceptance

You can see the overlap in the four lists as consensus that the process starts with validation and does have an end, thankfully. In between, the bites include anger and hurt and depression. Throughout many of these stages, the emotions can spike your cortisol, but the destruction from unresolved grief outweighs the benefit of going through momentary discomfort. The only way past grief is through it. No shortcuts.

Arriving at this first bite is usually delayed quite a bit, a year or more, after stopping the drinking. That's because while coming out of the acute stage of the disease into abstinence there's so much else going on. In that first year of sobriety, even if you've permitted yourself to believe you have losses, you're still swimming upstream against your physiology and your body's preference for alcohol. You're busy as hell swimming like hell. Once you're more established in sobriety, the swimming seems more manageable, so you can begin to feel grief, the noun, and begin grief, the process.

During the period of early sobriety an Alcoholic keeps hearing from himself and others that life goes on. Encouraging and well-intentioned. Sure beats You're Not Normal. I also heard that I would be the same person I've always been, only better without the booze. That's what they want to believe, but I know better, I know what I lost and the fallout I created. I'd like to buy into what they said about being the same person. The idea that you pick up and carry on with life just by quitting drinking seems so easy. It's called the Pollyanna Principle: The built-in capacity to dwell on the positive not the negative. The raw truth is that the negatives of the disease's impact and the losses it creates cannot be ignored. When the bottle goes away, it takes a whole piece of the Alcoholic's life, not just a small, inconsequential sliver of it. That needs validation. Parts of an Alcoholic's personhood are traumatically and efficiently lost to alcohol. Hopes, aspirations and reputations end. With Alcoholics these things don't die some quiet death by slinking under a rock and dying, they die in spectacular fireballs. It is a major loss to acknowledge and grieve; one Pollyanna cannot ignore.

Once you validate, the mourning process isn't necessarily easy or efficient or quick even if all the models have a progression. B.G. Simos, in *A Time to Grieve*, (Family Services Association of America, New York 1979) says after admitting you have a loss to grieve, "The process of grieving major loss takes at least two to four years." The longer you put off grieving, the longer it will take. The progression of bite after bite is so time consuming because a mourner has to close out or compartmentalize the old life and start a new one. An Alcoholic matures over time into a new life. Just like none of us became Alcoholic overnight, the new life doesn't come overnight either. Instant gratification doesn't go with recovery in general and with mourning specifically.

Of each of the four stressors, the stages of this one take the most time. Grieving feels like snail mail in these days of Instant Messages. But the sooner we identify and validate losses and the consequences of our disease and remission, the sooner we put a stamp on that letter.

You suffer the most from this stressor when you permit yourself to be caught between the hope that the loss will just go away on its own and the reality that it won't. Mourning can't start when you hang onto that Pollyannaish hope. The hope is the denial stage of each of the four models. Denial gets a horrible rap when it comes to Alcoholism, rehabilitation and recovery because it's usually pegged to denial that you have a problem. Denial is a term misused by those trying to convince anyone who misuses alcohol that they need help. These people who misuse the word around every alcohol-related problem are usually the same geniuses who believe shocking interventions are helpful. In reality, most people who misuse alcohol don't need help or the grief process for that matter because they are not Alcoholic. They are just garden-variety drunks. They don't need help for a drinking problem; they need only to stop being problem drinkers. Denial in the context of mourning is a different mechanism altogether. It is a completely normal, healthy and necessary part of grieving, not a barrier to getting help.

Denial functions as a buffer after the loss. During that time after the loss when you're so busy swimming just to stay abstinent, denial allows you to focus on the swimming, not the reasons why you are swimming. Two studies fifteen years apart demonstrate the value of denial as a temporary buffer. In 1968, Thomas Hacket of Harvard did a study of cardiac patients in a coronary care unit and found that cardiac patients have a higher survival rate when they minimize or deny their loss. In their cases the loss was their health, the first strand of the braid. In 1983, Richard Lazarus followed 61 patients who avoided asking about their impending surgeries. The 61 faced loss (again health) and denied it by ignoring their own questions. Lazarus found they fared better, with lower incidence of infection, fever and nausea, compared to patients who asked all the questions. Hacket's study was in the New England Journal of Medicine,

Lazarus' in *The Costs and Benefits of Denial*. (International University Press, New York) As long as you're not living permanently at this stage of grief, you are better off in your early recovery when you suspend reality a little. When you begin to notice the Symptoms of Sobriety, it's time to stop the denial and take a few more bites at mourning.

Alcoholics have a tendency to cling to their denial of their losses, not of their problem. By lingering in the stage, it only makes the cortisol worse. Even though the reason we linger in denial is simply that we don't want to feel worse, we're actually feeling worse because of the cortisol. To move away from more of continued Symptoms, the denial evolves into anger. Ashley Davis Prend identifies it as going from "Not me" to "Why me?" and it takes a long time. "On average it takes one to three years to work through the disorganization and anger stage. That's because you need to process the grief repeatedly so it can sink in, settling on deeper levels of consciousness over time."

Simply put, you're not going to be pissed off one time for one day, but you're entitled to it and it is a healthy part of what comes naturally during mourning and recovery. Different anniversaries rekinkle the anger. Social losses and financial ones have long tails and breed anger over and over. Impatience sparks the anger, too, because all of us Alcoholics have a little control freak in us. Unfortunately, some of us never get past the anger because that's where we lapse. We drink at the anger. Or if we don't drink, we become what's known as a dry drunk, a bitter and angry person who doesn't and won't drink. The dry drunk won't find recovery, but will maintain sobriety because they cling to the anger. They become dry drunks because of a false sense of power anger provides. It does beat being sad. Sad feels so broken, anger feels powerful, but sadness is the next stage. Rather than moving forward, the dry drunk chooses the power of anger rather than feeling like the ornament at the bottom of the Christmas storage box. They're usually more of a pain in the ass than they were when they were drinking.

When a person is mourning, an extremely critical concession needs to happen when he or she is at the anger stage in order to move to the sadness stage. We need to feel understood. As long as we feel we're not understood, we hang on to anger until someone concedes that they understand us. This is arguably the greatest benefit of 12-step meeting because people get your anger . . . they've got it, know exactly how it feels and want a way out. Conversely, when you feel misunderstood, as one would if coerced into going to the 12-step meeting, the anger lingers. Anger from this general feeling of being misunderstood is a messenger. "Just as physical pain tells us to take a hand off a hot burner, the pain of anger tells us a value has been compromised, changed or lost," according to Harriet Goldhor Lerner. (*The Dance of Anger*, Harper & Row, New York 1985) That anger is diffused and defused when someone understands us.

A rant levied at most Alcoholics is that we don't have any right to be angry. That's just insane. An Alcoholic is entitled to anger just like a non-Alcoholic. Anger over our losses is part of our healthy recovery. We have to have it. It's never okay for it to be directed at others, but anger at the loss in one of the strands, anger at the disease, anger at the humiliation endured from it, are all appropriate faces of constructive anger during the grief process.

Using Kubler Ross's five stages as a synopsis of the process it's important to note that the new stage doesn't mean you've left the old stage entirely. The grief process isn't so linear. You can go back and forth among the stages. They overlap, too.

Overlapping Stages of Grief

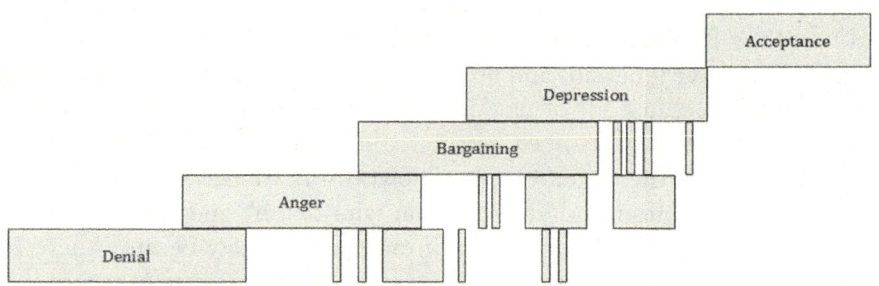

You could still feel anger later after you've entered other stages of reconstructing your life. Bargaining is a transitional stage. You're past denial, past most of the anger. Mentally or even verbally you address the "what ifs." "What if I move?" "What if I change careers?" "What if I try moderation?" (Save yourself the experiment: This one never works.) You get the what ifs because you're not quite at acceptance but you're closer to it than you were previously.

Depression and sadness are components of the process as well and in most of the models follow anger and bargaining. You're synthesizing loss. You're really Not Normal if you're not a little sad when looking at your losses. Pharmaceuticals can help with this stage. They're not a replacement for feeling the loss though. Any mourner, whether mourning a death in the family or the loss of a career, goes through a phase when you can't just smile away the loss. Sadness isn't morbid.

The good news about the sadness bite is that you can tacitly acknowledge, at last, that the loss is final. For a family member mourning a death, for example, it's here that it sinks in that so-and-so isn't coming home. For an Alcoholic, this is when it sinks in that what you lost is permanent. This is also the landmark point in which every Alcoholic has the realization that abstinence is the only solution. No more anger. No more bargaining.

The bad news is that the landmark is also the part of mourning where an Alcoholic is likely to lapse. We want to drink for the same reasons non-Alcoholics do . . . that it makes you feel good when you're sad or depressed. Alcohol soothes this way, and it seduces even non-Alcoholics at times of sadness. You're not really the first to be at this turning point, facing lapse or sadness as if there was no choice. One of the annoying traits of Alcoholics is that we feel we're so terminally unique and nobody ever felt what we're feeling at this stage of grief. Don't overthink it: We've all been here. Despite the darkness, realize that you now have most of the grief process is in your rearview mirror now. A drink would only start it over. There is recognizable life on the other side of the loss and you're closer to it at this stage. The successful recoverer sees it.

The duration of the depression depends only upon how resistant a mourner is to embracing realistic outcomes and embracing what we can glimpse as recognizable life on the other side of loss. Your life isn't going to be perfect. It wasn't before you stopped drinking either. When a griever welcomes the outcomes, this is the acceptance bite you've been working toward. There's a quiet expectation that things are and will be fine. That's all acceptance is. The end of the process isn't happiness or joy . . . it's just calmness.

No doubt spirituality has a role in the process. All four experts cited earlier spend dozens of pages on faith and the role of God or god. There isn't a religion on the planet without a grief ritual. If that works for you, awesome. It does for me, too, however in this frank discussion about Alcoholics and grief, I've left God out of it. If you're hinged to a higher power today in sobriety, it can speed up the grief process. Hopefully your connection to that higher power didn't begin with the prayer: Dear God, get me out of this one. A lot of Alcoholics think that constitutes spirituality.

A very effective way to tell where an Alcoholic is in the grief process is to witness their demeanor toward recovery. If he is passive, expecting recovery to just come on its own, he's at the denial part of the process. If he is active but not struggling with it, that's acceptance. At the start of the chapter I mentioned that you notice "something" in those who have the most experience in their recoveries. This is that something: Calmness. Acceptance. AA calls it serenity.

You're ready to move on from grief when you pay more attention to your environment than to yourself because the chaos of not be able to concentrate is gone. You're ready to move on from grief when you exchange questions for comments. The search for why indicates you're living in the past. You have grieved appropriately when you comment on how you'll use tomorrow. Staying perpetually in grief does not prove how sorry you are.

Failing to mourn condemns everyone but especially Alcoholics because of our hard-wired tendency toward lapse. We need genuine grief, and it doesn't need to be some huge public show. Genuine grief is the sobbing, sometimes silently, sometimes aloud, that expresses acceptance. That can happen at home, alone. You do the sobbing. When you do, the upshot is that you get to keep all the warmth and love that was always there underneath. Even on your worst days, it was always there. And it's yours again if you can accept one of the simplest, bluntest truths about recovery: We have to get over things and move on.

You don't get here automatically. Mourning is work. Time does not heal wounds all by itself. It takes work to grieve, more work than it does to process the other three stressors. "If you're not doing the necessary grief work of feeling, expressing and processing or if you're holding onto your grief, time alone will only exacerbate the problems," writes Prend. "Unresolved grief gets buried under anxiety, relationship problems and health problems." Like the Symptoms of Sobriety. So you can see why you can't simply not worry about it when it comes up. Which brings me back to Kermit Tyler and his horrible advice when he told someone, "Don't worry about it." Army Air Force First Lieutenant Tyler said those words to Joe Lockard, the 78th pursuit squadron's radar operator who spotted a large formation of incoming aircraft on screen in the pre-dawn hours of December 7, 1941. The Pearl Harbor Intercept Officer said, "Don't worry about it," instead of issuing a warning of the imminent attack, which consumed Pearl Harbor an hour later.

Chapter Eight

"Most of the time we don't communicate, we just take turns talking."—Unknown

All vertebrates have that flight-or-fight response as a survival mechanism, as mentioned earlier. It's our most basic and primitive coping skill for dealing with *physical* stressors since we lack cheetah speed or scales or quills or razor-like claws and teeth. Flight-or-fight is a lousy coping skill for the *emotional* stressors in the previous four chapters. We can't outrun shame . . . flight is out. And we can't stun our guilt into submission when it attacks us . . . fight is out. Evolution favored us though because we possess a tool to help battle against how the primitive cortisol makes us feel. That tool: Communication. It's only an effective cortisol solver if we use it.

A counselor told me, "It's probably a good thing you were in jail or you would have succeeded in your suicide plan. Jail saved your life." Which is not true. I countered, "If I wasn't in jail, I would have asked for help *and gotten it*." But that made me think, "Why then didn't I get help for my stresssors when they were bugging me?" Because I didn't want to bring the stressors out in the open for others to evaluate. I did not communicate.

I could have battled cortisol with a warm bath, which has been shown to lower cortisol in the bloodstream. How about preventing it from saturating the bloodstream to begin with? We have to communicate to solve the stressors and keep them from dumping the cortisol that causes the Symptoms. "The psychological rule," says Carl Jung, "is that when an inner situation is not made conscious, it happens outside as fate." Had I been half the communicator I think I am, had I only used this evolutionary leg-up, I would not have reached such a low bottom.

Improving your diet . . . getting more and better quality sleep . . . learning relaxation techniques . . . these are all fine Band-Aids for Alcoholics, but they don't fix problem stressors like guilt, shame, forgiveness and grief. The antidote to the cortisol is self-expression. Communicating.

If you're inclined instead to rely upon pharmaceuticals to help you through cortisol's effects, they are a mere bandage as well. And not a very effective one compared to better sleep or diet. Research by Gelpin and colleagues has shown that continuous use of benzodiazepines (commonly prescribed opiates used for overcoming the exaggerated startle response and mood changes associated with the Symptoms) did not reduce the Symptoms. Not to mention how dangerous benzos like Xanax and Valium are for Alcoholics. The pharmacy has no antidote. There's no pill, herb or supplement to reduce cortisol. The answer is communication.

When I read the Roosevelt quote, that's when I began to extract myself from my messy Symptoms, realizing I have to talk as a survival skill.

The V chart (APPENDIX I) demonstrates the progression of recovery up the right side of the illustration. You don't get any of these benefits of sobriety out of a workbook. You grow into the right side, overcoming the Symptoms of Sobriety by communicating when you feel yourself dipping back toward the center of the chart. Bradshaw says, "Only in the life of dialogue and communicating can we truly live and grow."

Having the stressors is not a defect. Not respecting them enough by talking through them is. That's because we're talking, in a way, about pain and not doing anything about pain *is* defective thinking. Being free of alcohol doesn't mean your pain and pressures disappear automatically. In actuality, some, like grief, reappear if you drank them away before. Alcoholics, some for the first time, face the pain of guilt or shame when the alcohol is gone. These may even have been the challenges leading to the Alcoholic drinking. When you get sober, you feel optimism and hope at first. It's called the Pink Cloud. Further into sobriety when old pains reveal themselves, you feel defeated and bleak because the stuff you fled under the influence is still there. It's Groundhog Day all over again. Until you get into the habit of talking through it.

Had I talked out my guilt and shame before they grew to critical levels, I would not have been so determined for many months to take my own life. I would have kept going up the right half of the chart and wouldn't have tripped down the dark rabbit hole I was in. And to rewind the tape even further, would I have lapsed at all if I had been assertively talking through my stressors? Certainly, no one would have had the illusion I was doing so well with my recovery. I cannot prove that things wouldn't have led to my bottom. It's an Ipse Dixit—Latin for an assertion without proof. I do not have studies or stats that bear out the assertion. Nor do I need to. I know it is no coincidence I am alive, as are millions with this disease, because I shunned isolation and communicated my stressors. That is evidence enough.

It is a suggestion of 12-steppers that spirituality is the antidote. In his memoir, *Decision Points*, (Crown Publishers, New York 2010) President George W. Bush credits God in his recovery. An alcohol abuser, not Alcoholic, he quit drinking for good decades before the White House years. "I believe God helped open my eyes, which were closing because of booze." At the other extreme are desperate Alcoholics who believe God is going to solve their problems for them and that the harder they thump the bible, the more Jesus will keep them sober. Belief works for a lot of people. I get that. Alcoholism, death and cancer all cause many spectacular collisions between belief (good things happen to good people) and reality (bad things happen to good people) and knowing a God helps many people through such collisions. It doesn't fix cortisol.

I'm not interested in dissuading anyone of the idea that spirituality *helps*. I'll respectfully leave that decision to you. I grew up in a Catholic household, lost my faith completely, regained it without organized religion, lost it again, became spiritual yet again, prayed often, then never . . . so I know what a challenge spirituality can be. I've tried virtue and I've tried it my way. It works when I don't do things my way . . . but that's just for me. I'm comfortable today in my own spirituality knowing there is a higher power and I'm not him. Such acceptance doesn't help the cortisol the way communication does. Our troubles with grief, guilt, shame and forgiveness are of our own making because we fail at communicating as a coping skill, not because we fail at faith. Faith-based programs succeed in ways secular ones (especially criminal justice ones) do not. Neither works without communications. A number of studies document the correlation between life-long wellness and spirituality: This isn't one of them. Instead, what my research indicates is that what is proven and indispensable is the communication part of recovery programs. Divine relationships transform many lives, but you still need help with the humans.

We need to talk.

Real talk. Not tweets or emails; live communication instead of social media gadgetry. Face-to-face communication is a skill we don't do well as a society, not just as Alcoholics. The impression is that we are a more connected culture these days . . . The reality is that we are more isolated than ever. A human connection with eye contact and gestures is gradually being usurped by impersonal devices. *I-disorders* are what author Larry Rosen calls the communications distraction and overload of technology. "It's gone past the stage of, 'This might be a problem,' to 'It is a problem for many.'" (*USA Today*, 3/27/12) For information and connectivity, we've got some amazing tools. We don't use any of them successfully as therapeutic weapons in recovery because they don't replace face-to-face.

I'll make only one entirely speculative statement in this book and that is as we see the Millennial Generation—the one feasting the most at the table of social media and electronics—get older, their generation will be the one with the greatest problem with Alcohol Use Disorders compared to other generations in U.S. history. Percentage-wise, the Millennials will still have the same eight percent affected by Alcoholism and 28 percent struggling (or not) with Alcohol Abuse. But the severity and duration will be worse, in my opinion, because of their preference for impersonal communication. Consider the financial impact of Alcohol Use Disorders today and play that tape forward, the cost will be devastating, the personal and family suffering, immeasurable. I hope I am wrong.

To heal toxic shame or ease Symptoms of Sobriety, we need to externalize what gives us the cortisol out face-to-face. We need to bring our disruptions out into the daylight and debrief others on our wants, needs and hurts. That stuff we don't talk about? We need to talk about. When we do, we learn it's okay to be human. We're only as sick as our secrets.

With skyrocketing cortisol in play, an Alcoholic is closer to the next drink than the last one. Communication may be the only way out. Yet we get an injury like guilt or shame and what we do as Alcoholics is clam up. We feel we simply cannot afford to risk communicating more vulnerabilities than we've already exposed. Instinctively, we want to flee the threat. The more the public stigma leads to shame, the more Fight-or-Flight makes us want to withdraw from their contact. As lousy as I said other people are for your recovery in the chapter on shame, we *need* other people to get well. We need their communication and ours. It is a human nature nearly as ancient as Fight-or-Flight.

The times we want to flee and when being a lone wolf seems to be appealing are precisely the times we need other people. It sounds counterintuitive because a faulty connection to other people has fed into our cortisol problem. However, we're in the most danger as Alcoholics when we shut down communication. Those times are the ones we most need to get a sense of our place among other people, to hear their tales and to hear we belong because their tales are our tales, too. We need the pack, not being the loner. In the wild, the lone wolf is the one howling because he needs the *answering cry*. That beast gives us a valuable lesson about how critical our connection to other people is and how sad the days are without the connection.

The catch is that you need people you can count on. More on that toward the end of the book.

The fact is we need five things to keep us on the right half of the chart in APPENDIX I and out of trouble.

Friendship.
Acceptance.
Intimacy.
Consistency.
And Responsibility.

We can have none of those five without people on whom we can rely and the communication we share with them. Two studies bear this out: The most recent (June 2010) is from the Center for the Study of Addiction and Recovery at Texas Tech University. This work demonstrated that those who dealt with stress by avoiding it had twice the frequency of alcohol cravings compared to people who used communication strategies to confront and understand stress. The second study is more general. The work of psychologist James Pennebaker ("Disclosure of Trauma and Immune Functions: Health Implications for Psychotherapy," in *Journal of Consulting and Clinical Psychology*, 1988) demonstrated that 25 men and women who suddenly suffered a major loss remained healthier after six months if they talked to others about their tragedies than if they did not communicate. People who talked through feelings about life even had better immune response, fewer trips to the doctor, fewer health complaints and fewer drugs prescribed compared to people who talked only about superficial, neutral life events. Pennebaker also detailed the results in his own book nearly a decade later. (*Opening Up*, The Guilford Press, New York 1997)

At life's intersections, if we don't communicate well with others and do it with specificity and substance, we're going to get t-boned.

If communicating feels one-sided at first, you're doing it right. It has to be one-sided and you may feel like you're just taking. It *is* all about the Alcoholic. And it has to be, at least at first. AA and other recovery resources will point out that in early recovery anything you put ahead of your sobriety you *will* lose. Davis Prend adds, "In the beginning . . . a definite period of self-absorption is necessary. In some ways you have to be completely, narcissistically involved in order to activate the healing process." You're not really in a position to give to others until you give to yourself first.

Communication is the glue that holds an Alcoholic together during recovery, so in that regard it *is* me-oriented. In no way does this mean exalting yourself or venting your ego. Instead, the emphasis is on self-disclosure. Self-disclosure is the give-and-take even though it might feel like you're just taking.

We have a bandage of silence over the wounds alcohol left if we clam up. The bandage does not cure the cortisol, it only makes the Symptoms feel less goofy temporarily. Self-disclosure is the medicine for the cortisol.

"Disclosing private information about ourselves is a very effective assertiveness skill. Private feelings and worries cannot be dealt with by other people by denying or disregarding the truths of your feelings," according to psychologist Smith. "The type of voluntary self-disclosure is about things we assume we should hide." Like grief. Like guilt. "Voluntary self-disclosure is not to be confused with the vomiting up of confessions of lack of self-worth." Voluntary self-disclosure also means talking only about *today*. AA: "Unless some good or useful purpose is to be served, past occurrences should not be discussed." Talk about what you feel, in other words, not what you did.

Smith adds that his work reveals that you don't have to worry about more stigma or ridicule for putting your feelings out there. "Your voluntary disclosure of negative factors about yourself and your own ready acceptance of them is probably the most potent and effective assertiveness skill in preventing manipulation and assuring your own peace of mind."

Pennebaker says communication has to be about substance, not chit-chat . . . Davis Prend says it needs to be somewhat selfish, not in a rude or uncaring way, but an orientation inward toward your needs and goals in sobriety . . . And Smith has introduced the idea of assertiveness.

Assertiveness is the Arcanum Arcanorum—the secret of secrets—of Alcoholic relapse prevention. The myth today is that every Alcoholic who is grieving or feels guilty, every one of us who's shamed or humiliated, should feel that way. Our voiceboxes should be cauterized, our spines removed, and we have to be meek, servile and benign. We are erroneously expected to be funereal, subdued and passive. No Alcoholic will survive under this myth. No Alcoholic is going to get his recovery handed to him, but he doesn't stand a chance to get his life if he doesn't take it back and that means being assertive. You have to take back communication, take back a right to say, "NO," take back a right to not be badgered, take back a right to change your mind. Alcohol did not change these benefits of humanness, and you don't have to apologize for assertively taking them back.

Being assertive allows us to: A) relay our thoughts, feelings and beliefs; B) in a manner of civility and tact; C) without remorse, reluctance or shyness; and D) with credibility (a commodity normally denied Alcoholics). If you have C) and remain reluctant or bashful, that's a communication barrier and a recovery barrier. Social insecurity is, after all, a reason why some non-Alcoholics drink and a trigger for some of us. Alcohol is liquid courage. Another paradox of alcohol. Courage in communication might be attained more safely by focusing on how we do A) and B) and the trick to courage is assertiveness. We learn to say "Who the hell are you to judge me?" without the arrogance of actually saying those words.

Fogging discussed earlier is one tool. It helps defend your right to be your own judge without being defensive and without taking on more of the shame that destabilizes your cortisol. You keep yourself healthier and your recovery healthier by being assertive, which has an added benefit of desensitizing yourself from shame. You also desensitize yourself to criticism from people you care about while disarming the ones you don't really care about and who don't care about you.

Unless we learn assertive ways of A), cortisol will still get the best of us because we are not communicating our boundaries. If we cannot refuse the requests or impositions of others who demand a right to grant us forgiveness, we live on their agendas. If we're not saying, "No," to them, we're saying it to ourselves. Being assertive allows us to avoid internalizing too much guilt or shame or grief, creating that same squirrel cage, feedback loop of cortisol begetting more cortisol.

Assertiveness is not aggressiveness. Aggression means you are inclined toward hostile behaviors. Assertiveness means you are inclined only toward confidence and self-assuredness, two things at the hub of successful recovery.

Assertive vs. Aggressive

An aggressor steps up for himself or his beliefs in a way prone to stepping on the beliefs of others. It results in anger. It can also bring on more guilt if you're not some sort of sociopath. Why create more guilt? An assertive person steps up for himself and his beliefs by expressing them in helpful and direct ways. Neither aggression nor assertiveness guarantee "winning" but aggression makes sure there will be a loser. Aggression also diminishes a person's credibility... assuming we have any.

There is a third alternative: Passive behavior. However, as an Alcoholic in sobriety you cannot afford to be meek and withdrawn, overlooked and walked upon. The passive don't communicate. (Passive-aggressive is not a fourth alternative, but is a psychological disorder to be avoided. Who hasn't thought of dropping of a ton of pennies to pay their mortgage? It's ok to think it, but a constant pattern of intentionally creating inefficiency for people who piss you off is a recognized disorder. Passive-aggressive communication willfully makes more work/effort/problems for ourselves—getting that many pennies isn't easy—by getting back at someone with intentional inefficiency, a tactic the twisted use to make more work for people confronting them. That's a low-payoff, warped way of thinking, not a communication style.)

Here are contrasts of the three styles:

- If you are criticized for being Alcoholic, the passive person takes it, sits and fumes silently, and maybe reads some infernally campy Erma Bombeck book to ease his angst. The aggressive person shouts and rants, maybe socks the clown in the melon. The assertive person responds, "I'm working on it. I'm even interested in helping you learn more about it if you're interested."
- If you lapse and someone calls you out, the passive person looks downward and takes his lumps. The aggressive person points fingers and snaps or storms off. The assertive person looks the other person in the eye and agrees to the facts and says, "My plan is . . ."

The casual observation of group therapy participants shows the need for those struggling with lapse or relapse to be assertive. Nine of ten are defensively aggressive, because louder makes them more right, or acquiescently passive, because being quieter means they are more sorry. Only one in 10 hasn't shelved his assertiveness skills.

There's an easy way to begin incorporating assertiveness. Start with the non-verbals. Sixty percent of communication is non-verbal. Instinctively, humans pick up on non-verbal codes and interpret them without having been formally trained to do so. This fact helps explain why there are so many misunderstandings via electronic messaging: We cannot hear the inflection or see the body language. It's easy to guillotine someone in a text but not eye-to-eye. The non-verbals that say aggressive vs. assertive:

Non-Verbal Cues

Aggressive	Assertive
Loud voice	Firm but warm voice
Piercing eyes	Gentle eye contact
Hands clenched, on hips or pointing	Relaxed hands
Arms crossed	Loose posture
Invades personal space	Leans into conversation

In TV news, as interviewers, we watch a guest for these cues which can also signal a guest's veracity, plus we watch ourselves to police out our own aggressive non-verbals, the ones that tend to turn off viewers. To show how non-verbals, especially aggressive ones, communicate and possibly contradict the actual words, consider Arizona Governor Jan Brewer and President Barack Obama. In January 2012, she welcomed the President to her state. She greeted him as he deplaned Air Force One. As they talked on the tarmac away from microphones, Brewer pointed a finger at the President as a mom scolds. Obama had a look on his face as if he just sucked a lemon as he looked at the aggressive gesture. To the millions of onlookers who saw the image over the next week, whatever was coming out of her mouth when she pointed became irrelevant. Still is. More importantly, her credibility took a hit.

Watch how you talk. Literally. Use a mirror to see how you use body language. One thing especially important to watch is eye contact. Alcoholics are especially poor at looking into a mirror, and that's not a metaphor, I mean actually looking at our reflections. We just don't do it much in sobriety and psychologists can't seem to figure out if it is because we're that unhappy with our physical appearances or if there's some deeper reason tied to denial, morality or honesty. Either way, the Alcoholic in us wishes the image in the mirror would just stay there after we walked away. And now we don't study that image in a mirror, yet it's a simple way to check assertiveness skills. Do your eyes look away while you brush your teeth? You won't encourage people to look you in the eye if you're unwilling to look into your own. It will not matter what you say or how sincere you are when your eye contact is a bad non-verbal. Your chances of communicating what you want about the stressors in your life is very low if eye contact isn't there. People will hear one thing but decide another about you based on your non-verbals, just like Brewer was only commenting on the President's plane ride, not his policies. If the messages don't match each other, people go with the body language. By the way, that is precisely why so many people saw through the bologna you were trying to sell back in your drinking days: Your non-verbals overtook your lies.

Lack of eye contact, the most common non-verbal tell, is a learned avoidance response. We learn to avoid eye contact without being aware of it, says Smith. "In the past, when we made eye contact in a conflict and not coped well with the conflict, the other person made us nervous. Without realizing it, to reduce the nervousness, we shift our focus away from a person making us uncomfortable and that makes us feel better, at least temporarily. After a while of successfully avoiding nervousness, not looking someone in the eye becomes a habit." Ronald and Patricia Potter-Efron, in *Letting Go of Shame*, (Hazelden, Center City, MN 1989) agree with Smith. "Shame drives down a person's head and eyes. Nevertheless, the person who's face flushes with shame is also someone who wants and needs to learn how to hold her head up again in calm dignity and realistic pride."

This is the easiest of your non-verbal habits to fix, though most people find it hard to look someone in the eye directly and maintain concentration. With a mirror and really minimal practice, you can improve your assertiveness, your message and your concentration.

The mirror also is helpful for seeing how you lean into a conversation as well as whether or not you keep your chin level. Alcoholics develop a habit of backing away from instead of leaning into a conversation, as well as burying our chins in our chests . . . all techniques we tried to keep people from detecting alcohol on our breaths.

Also practice doing something with your hands. If you are prone to nervous trembling or pointing or clenching your fists, pinch your left pinky between your right thumb and index finger. This is another on-camera trick. Practice it even when you are sitting idly. It becomes second nature when you're engaged in a real conversation.

This small bit of communication instruction on assertiveness, eye contact and other non-verbals is just a quick-fix and are not all-inclusive remedies. The focus here is more on the "why to" rather than the "how to."

Think of communication as a valuable preventive, too, not just a coping response. If you implement a couple of these assertive tactics, they can help prevent the cortisol. They'll also be useful when you're in a crisis with the Symptoms, but if you're engaging in healthy, supportive dialogue, it helps keep you from getting close to the edge to begin with. It's worthwhile to remember there are unreasonable people, antagonistic people, rude people and people of questionable intelligence everywhere and you *have* become a target for them. You haven't given them permission to badger you. The assertive response: "I wish you'd stop pressuring me." Lean into it. Look them in the face. No guilt. No shame. That's what I mean by this being preventive.

If other people react to your assertive self-disclosure about your stressors by trying to convince you you have no right to feel the way you do, your reply is simple and direct: "You're correct. That's still the way I feel." That person, if a safe person for you, must respond to you on the same level of honest and personal feelings or you just don't deal with them at all. That's also preventive. You're stopping them from shaming. When faced with critique or criticism, ask the speaker for their specific suggestions on how they think you can improve. It is remarkable how the simple but assertive move disarms critics. That's preventive.

Once drinking stops, alcohol can no longer take away your capability to discern safe people from the unsafe, the valuable critique from the valueless criticism. Unsolicited advice sucks, especially when you're working hard to keep recovering, and it is okay to disregard critics. You take what you can use. Critics who live in the past, label or judge you . . . you cannot use them. They will always put a premium on what you did, and meet your assertiveness with determination to prove you're still bad.

In relapse prevention, guilt, shame, forgiveness issues or grief don't just disappear because you have learned how to communicate. They simply lose much of their power over you because you are taking back your power. Strategically finding the right venue in which to take back your power is the next step.

Chapter Nine

"Why drag about the corpse of your memory? Bring the past to judgment into the thousand-eyed present and live ever in a new day."—Ralph Waldo Emerson

Improving assertiveness and communication are the secrets to succeeding in sobriety. You have to do it out loud, though, not just between the covers of a book or in the sanctuary of your home. Put it into live practice. Moving from a social arena of dozens of monologues with no dialogue to an arena of healthy exchange puts you in a good position to thwart the Symptoms of Sobriety.

The Pennebaker study in general and the fact I've quoted so many psychologists may lead you to believe I'm talking only of psychotherapy as that healthy exchange. Yes and no. Ultimately I *am* talking about day-to-day interaction, but to get there, individual therapy, group therapy and group self-help are effective resources most successfully recovering Alcoholics tap. The controlled environments are one way to meet the more intensive communication needs before trying out our new skills on the public at large, especially if we've pushed away from public interaction for a while. I'm interested in the benefits of one-to-one counseling, but I'll only cover that briefly next. Most of this chapter and the next cover group therapy and group self-help, because there's a lot that can go wrong there and there's a ton of misinformation on each. First, one-to-one counseling.

Therapy, or counseling, is not for answers why Alcoholics drink. Every therapist will give you a different answer suited to their own bias and their own specialty. It is a disease. That's enough explanation. The value of counseling is unquestioned in the treatment of patients with the disease, just like it is for people suffering with cancer, not for the answer to "why" but for how to live with it and communicate through it.

Non-Alcoholics see a therapist for change. Alcoholics see a therapist to see a therapist. To talk. We know there is no changing the disease. Instead of change-making, counseling is people-providing. There's no miracle transformation when you leave the office: You're still Alcoholic. But you've bettered your assertiveness skills, your communication.

People-providing probably does not require professional assistance, however, too much is at stake when you struggle with sobriety to leave it to anyone but a pro. At least at first. And one-to-one is a safe first step. If you can afford it or have insurance to cover it, one-to-one counseling is the most value you can purchase for your recovery.

Therapists have their critics but I'm not one of them. I have not met anyone, Alcoholic or non-Alcoholic who couldn't stand to gain from talking with a professional. Hell, 74 percent of therapists have been or are in therapy! (W.E. Henry, *The Fifth Profession*, Jossey-Bass, San Francisco, CA 1971) Even when life is good it can still have its slushy spots. Talking through them with a pro is critical to success in recovery. Therapy is not precise science and results only matter if *you* feel them. That is what will define a pro. Opponents of Behavioral Therapy *as an Alcoholism treatment* have produced enough evidence—to be discussed later—to discredit therapists and counselors using the methods *for Alcoholism*. No one has ever found fault with the people-providing benefit of talking to a counselor.

Not everyone is at ease being verbal at first with a counselor. So write to yourself first. You may discover value in journaling on an ongoing basis, but at a minimum, writing down your feelings before the counseling helps you focus. You can write down your feelings of your last drink, your first weeks without, the Symptoms you're feeling, or your anxiety over talking to a shrink. It's not about paragraphs or pages or punctuation. Writing helps you put yourself over your disease, establishing your superiority over it, because you realize a consciousness you never had while drinking. When you read what you wrote, you will understand what I mean.

The guru you select will advise you to ignore: Most criticisms and blames for what you're feeling; unsolicited obligations; accidental mistakes or mistakes no one can correct; ignorant behavior; inefficient conduct; unavoidable loss; and human imperfection. Those were the easy things to talk about, right? Spend your time instead talking *specifically* about what is eating you before it swallows your sobriety whole. That's the hard part. We're reluctant to self-disclose and talk about intense feelings because we're Alcoholic and we used to drink over them rather than talk, afraid we'll be judged or sound like we're nuts. No therapist will say you're nuts if you talk about your feelings, they might say you're nuts if you don't because you have a lot to lose to the Symptoms. What you feel is what *you* feel. The therapist's chair will validate that.

My own therapist was Jack Daniel's of Lynchburg for several years. He never validated a thing. Invalidated a lot, like my two marriages, a pretty decent career and lifestyle, relationships with family and friends. Then again, we never talked.

Be prepared to talk. We can speak 125 words per minute but can hear 400-600 words per minute. Nobody understands that equation and the value of listening better than a therapist. Listening is the skill a therapist leases to you, along with their objectivity. Your role is to talk. The therapist listens and helps you put your stressors into perspective.

There's a whole river of grievances and tensions underlying every visit made to a therapist.

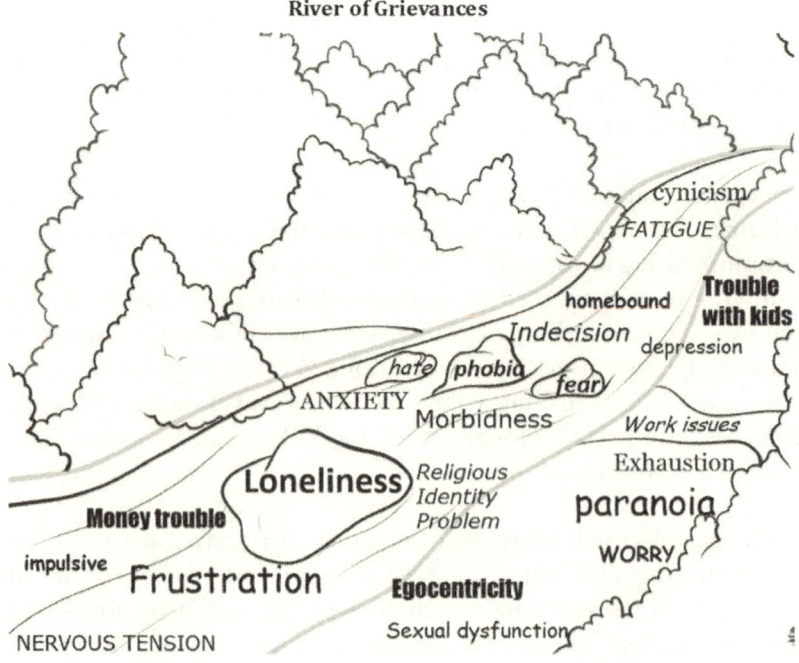

One or more of the four stressor underlies each of these things floating in the river. When you are in the river, you see it only from the canoe. A therapist sees it from an aircraft, knowing where it is going and what's beyond the bends you can't see, whether what lies ahead are calm waters or rapids. Trust the perspective. Most accredited professionals will help you navigate the river from that unique vantage point, even those pros who have no expertise in Alcoholism. It is my view, however, that an Alcoholic in sobriety needs a therapist who has Alcoholism and alcohol abuse credentials and not just a general familiarity with the two Alcohol Use Disorders. If your river is the Mississippi, you're not going to benefit much from a river expert who knows only the Nile.

Some have Substance Abuse Training, but ask specifically about Alcoholism. That doesn't insure you against the therapist's personal bias. It does ensure that the person with whom you are working understands you have a medical condition and your success or failure in handling your stressors can have grave medical consequences compared to a non-Alcoholic with the same stressors. Most gurus list their specialties. If they have seven different ones listed (children, marriage, anger management, etc.) they won't be terrible. You need a rifle, though, not an ammo wagon.

Many psychiatrists, social workers, psychologists and counselors believe they know a great deal more about Alcoholism than they actually do. They complete their training largely unprepared to deal with Alcoholic patients. Wilson-Schaef says, "Most mental health professionals have had a unit on Alcoholism and/or addiction. That makes us even more dangerous. We have just enough knowledge to think we know something.

"Traditional mental health techniques and theories have been singularly unsuccessful in the treatment of Alcoholism."

Ronald Rogers and Chandler McMillin add, "Many treat Alcoholism as a result of underlying psychological problems, not as its own disease . . . that's the worst approach you can take." (*Relapse Traps*, Bantam Books, New York 1991)

Even if you are only there for the people-providing, be aware of the biases, not just personal ones but ones due to the therapist's training. This is especially a concern if your appointments are subject to criminal justice or Employee Assistance Program (EAP) reporting: You may be the patient, but you are not the client. You'll want to find additional people-providing in addition to what you do for compliance. A social worker once told me, point blank, "Because we work with law breakers, we don't know when they're not lying." Hardly, bias-free . . . or therapeutic.

A therapist who is in recovery himself or herself is a bonus. (If he or she claims never to have lapsed, doubt this claim.) To continue the river analogy, the person not only has the vantage of seeing the river from a plane, they've been in the canoe, too. Anyone can understand crumpled cars and broken bones. To understand crumpled spirits and broken beliefs you need someone who's been through it. You have to have experience to know what experience is. A lifetime of conceptualization will not match the range of data supplied by living through a life similar to your own. Textbooks or classrooms cannot let anyone feel what you're feeling.

If their memories are your memories, if they've felt what you've felt, the perspective they can bring to your people-providing has amazing credibility. Wilson Schaef adds, "We simply cannot underestimate the healing effects of being with other persons who struggled with the same problems."

Sometimes a paraprofessional—a counselor rather than a therapist—may be more accessible cost-wise and schedule-wise. They might not have had the training of a psychologist but have a passion for helping Alcoholics, and almost without exception are in recovery themselves. So they do have perspective. Albert Einstein revolutionized physics. That wasn't his training. He was a mathematician, and postal clerk before that. Alfred Kinsey wrote the most thorough book on human sexuality ever published. He was an entomologist: A bug scientist. The people who work in Alcoholology who are likely to have the next breakthrough are probably the ones least formally trained in traditional medicine or psychology because, like Einstein, they don't wear the blinders of the beliefs of a degree program or the beliefs of the instructors who trained them. The most widespread, and some would argue the most successful, approach to drinking problems was developed by Bill Wilson, a stockbroker, not an alcohol expert. Paraprofessionals don't have to be an authorities to have the authenticity.

Training alone does not make or break a leader. There are three types of leadership: Traditional—like a parent; Bureaucratic—legal; or Charismatic. Recovery flourishes only under Charismatic leadership. Authenticity. The powerplays of the justice system's adversarial "treatment" programs are the exception because the counselors sometimes do have the charisma, but the seat of their leadership is bureaucratic only. And coerced. No amount of charisma will overcome that, and the abject failure of criminal justice programs is proof that bureaucratic approaches don't produce anything resembling recovery.

There's a great February 1965 *Psychiatry* magazine article (Matthew Lipman and Salvatore Pizzurro, "Charismatic Participation in the Social Process") demonstrating specifically why charismatic counselors or therapists succeed in helping prevent lapse. The article was preceded by Max Weber's "From Max Weber—Essays in Sociology." (Oxford University Press, New York 1958) The gist of both works is that no Alcoholic is looking for a magician, simply an individual gifted in sharing values and opportunities with others and who's talented enough to listen as well as speak. The charismatic counselor has a big ear, not a big mouth.

I didn't think I'd need to mention that compassion is another trait to require of a counselor. Seems pretty obvious. But then I heard a counselor verbally slug someone below the belt at a group therapy session. She told a patient his son was her job security during the patient's introduction in front of the entire crowd. Not charisma, not compassion. That's a big mouth and no ears. What the patient could have begun, instead of being stung, was to interpret the meaning of incidents of his life, like the dreams he has for his son.

Talking to a gifted person, you'll likely arrive at the conclusion that the degree of damage to yourself and/or others is not the scorched earth you think it is and that there is order despite alcohol's chaos and the Symptoms. Sometimes we need to hear ourselves out loud. We hear there is an end that isn't tragic. You begin to believe that with someone with charisma. You benefit from hearing yourself tell *your* story until you know how you *feel* about your story. You hear how guilt or shame or grief or forgiveness impact how you feel today when you say it out loud. Hearing it between your own ears over and over continues to poison you, hearing it come out of your mouth helps you convince yourself that the damage is passed.

It's more economical to find such a valuable opportunity to hear yourself while still benefiting from a paraprofessional with authenticity in group therapy. Group therapy and group self-help are not the same thing. Group therapy is led by a professional or paraprofessional and is not free. Group self-help meetings are free—donation expected—and are not supervised by a therapist or counselor. Direct feedback is encouraged in group therapy since there is someone trained to lead or steer (or referee) the discussion. Cross-talk doesn't fly at group self-help. In fact, you'd probably be best avoiding the self-help meetings where it is encouraged. These "fixers" are co-dependents-in-training, insisting upon critiquing your sobriety not working their own program.

In *The Shrinking of America*, (Little, Brown and Co., Boston, MA 1983) clinical psychologist Bernie Zilbergeld points out "Most people are basically healthy and resourceful . . . and are not, as we now seem to believe, in need of constant monitoring and fixing up by behavioral experts." They are well-suited for group self-help. Those looking for more guidance on what to do, they are well-suited for group therapy. Sometimes we need the guidance after going one-to-one with our effort on communicating our stressors, sometimes we don't need it.

Watch out for group therapy that emphasizes a "hot seat" approach: Break-them-down confrontational techniques have not been proven clinically. Sometimes the public view of the Alcoholic person only as a fun-loving, thrill-seeking, irresponsible and childish person who is into the immediate gratification of every impulse is interpreted in group-therapy circles are a need to punish it out of him. Humiliate him. Teach him a lesson. That's where this obnoxious hot-seat idea originated. However, the self-willed jerk just described is the alcohol abuser, not the Alcoholic. Behavioral approaches can work for alcohol abusers because lapse, in their world, is based on how they *want* to behave, not how they are feeling. For Alcoholics, it is a different matter. For Alcoholics, "Cognitive [Behavioral] treatment is not adequate for recovery," says Wilson-Schaef. "To deal only with the analytical, rational and logical is to perpetuate the disease."

No one can knock Behavioral Therapy in general because it works very well for a lot of *behavioral* problems, like alcohol abuse, overeating or kleptomania. No one can knock its founder, Albert Ellis: Only the Gideons and the phone company have their names on more books. Ellis is to psychology what Lawrence Tribe is to law. But Alcoholism is not a *behavior*.

When you hear Behavioral Therapy in conjunction with group therapy, think of conditioning, like B.F. Skinner's strategies training pigeons or Ivan Pavlov's dogs trained to drool at the sound of a dinner bell. Behavioral Therapy uses the theory on people. (Here's a funny thought to ponder: Did Pavlov condition his dogs? Or did the dogs condition Pavlov to feed them?) Brainwashing is an accurate but out-of-favor synonym. There is no room for emotion. "This myopia," says William Lewis, "May stem from a standpoint which originated in a laboratory where experimental animals were to be manipulated, not loved."

("Why People Change," in *The Psychology of Influence*, Holt, Rinehart and Winston, Inc., New York 1972)

You are retrained overtly and covertly in Behavioral Therapy. You are taught to act. Therefore, you become a superior actor, ignoring the accuracy of the script. You play a role and pass the program. You cannot move from sobriety to recovery by acting. Teaching grade schoolers to the standardized tests they're administered is an appropriate comparison. They can pass the test taken and still fail to learn anything of use in practical, everyday life.

Zen Buddhists are more obvious in their behavioral tactics. The Zen Master carries a wooden staff with which he'll cut through the emotion or philosophizing of his pupil by whacking him suddenly and unexpectedly upside the head while yelling, "Kwats!" The pupil is brought into compliance quickly and clearly without explanation or hope for one because there is nothing to be explained. Behavioral Therapy works the same way without the wooden staff. A harsh intervention might just be appropriate for the abuser to take him down a notch or two. It is wholly inappropriate for the Alcoholic who is already stretched tight with grief, shame and guilt. Alcoholism doesn't respond to bullying. The Symptoms don't respond to bullying. Does grief? Any of the other stressors? Who is the harshness for anyway? Rubbing a puppy's nose in his own shit when he dumps on the floor never taught a dog anything but usually made the master feel a little better. This is not charismatic leadership.

"I know of no valid treatment technique that requires people to be treated disrespectfully and without due consideration for their rights as humans," Zilbergeld adds. If you're on the hot seat for what you've communicated, how willing are you going to be to keep communicating? Terence Gorski agrees in his landmark book, *Staying Sober*. (Herald House/ Independence Press, Independence, MO 1986) "I quickly learned that confrontation would not work with relapse-prone patients because one thing they had experience with more than anything else was confrontation."

The confrontation tactic uses shame as a lever. The disconnect is obvious. If an Alcoholic lapses because of shame, shaming him more won't prevent another lapse. Be aware that a great many public taxpayer funded group therapy programs use the tactic. The clinical supervisor at a 300 bed facility headed up a program of her own design that was 20 years behind the times when she started it ten years earlier. She's known for screaming at people on the hot seat. She told a 46-person unit she was surprised none earned an "intervention" lately . . . "You guys are slick," she told them . . . as if they were violating written or unwritten rules by accomplishing what they were supposed to accomplish. Nine days later, eight of them had been hot-seated. Her program routinely shamed the participants right up to their graduation from the six-month program. "Your best thinking is what got you here." An average of three participants quit the program before getting that final shaming on graduation. Of the seven lucky enough to hear it, five lapse within the first year. Would the public program have a higher success rate if the patients were instead told "Your *worst* thinking got you here, a disease helped you into your worst thinking?" In contrast, other programs, mostly private, have a ritual at graduation from group called a "cupping ceremony." Each treatment completer decorates a coffee cup and gives a speech about their journey as they depicted it on the cup. Counselors and peers give some constructive feedback and the cup is hung on the wall. A year later, if you are still sober, you reclaim your mug. Seven of ten are still sober.

The notion that an Alcoholic gets "more better" in group therapy by stripping away dignity is complete nonsense. Manipulating a person and doing so without compassion or kindness or regard for basic civility and calling it rehabilitative is shocking, backward and barbaric. Is this really where we are in public health? Someday we are going to view the interventional style of Behavioral Therapy *for Alcoholism* in the 20th century as the same quackery as leeches in the 18th century and phrenology in the 19th. Behavior Therapy *for Alcoholism* diminishes the current science on a disease in favor of unproven (or worse, disproven) theories. "The confrontational and punitive tactics have not proved to be superior to other more conventional helping behaviors of counselors, social workers and mental health professionals," concluded William Cloud and Robert Granfield. (*Recovery from Addiction*, New York University Press, New York 2001) The Behavioral Therapy theories have only been proven effective with alcohol abusers and illicit drug users and other antisocial or deviant behaviors.

Confrontational group therapy is NOT better than no group therapy at all. It is a deterrent to ever getting more treatment and upsets any positive a person gained from one-to-one counseling. The pursuit of good ends does not justify the employment of bad means: This conclusion is backed up in Timothy O'Farrell's and W. Fals-Stewart's "Alcoholism Services Research in the Managed Care Era," in *Recent Developments in Alcoholism*, vol. 15, 2001.

Group therapy is usually used before or in addition to getting into group self-help. Many of us benefit from one or the other rather than both, but 12-step meetings have a much wider availability and for that reason are more popular. The Substance Abuse and Mental Health Services Administration (SAMHSA) in 2008 reported an annual average of five million people 12 and older attended a group self-help meeting in the prior 12 months. One third also went for one-to-one counseling or group therapy. Because AA is so widespread, most one-to-one and group therapy is based on the 12-steps and those counselors encourage participating in self-help to boost sobriety. In fact, the 1998 National Treatment Center Study Summary Report from the University of Georgia found 90 percent of 450 treatment centers are based on the 12 steps, while 10 percent rely on Behavior Therapy.

The National Institute on Alcohol Abuse and Alcoholism (NIAAA) seems to endorse the 12-step approach in group therapy as well. In 2008, it found Behavioral Therapy less successful than 12-step methods. "Individuals in 12-step oriented therapy have increased subsequent AA participation and it is the AA involvement that leads to better outcomes by buffering the effects of social pressures to drink. AA exposes a person to a network of people who have a goal of sobriety and support one another in achieving that goal."

Group therapy requires signing up and showing up. Group self-help requires only showing up. One thing to note though, if it is confidentiality you seek, one-to-one counseling is the only route 100 percent confidential. Group therapy has a large degree of confidentiality, too. Group self-help has no such assurance. Anonymous is not a synonym for confidential. Ask yourself, though, does recovery really need to be confidential? Far too many get ticklish about talking "publicly" about their shame and other stressors. The alternative is not talking. Twelve-step meetings are not the town newspaper. Even if it was, some of our under-the-influence feats were more public than anything you'd say in a group self-help meeting ever would be.

These are safe venues in which to communicate. They consist of people who share the exact same struggles as you. They've been told You're Not Normal, too. Talking things out among them is cathartic. You don't need to talk about every confession you have. You don't get style points for deeper traumas. You do get style points for creating a climate of trust by putting on the table the things that are giving you the Symptoms. We risk reaching out because we need a new label, a new place to belong, and there is safety among others who are also trying to shed old labels and stressors. If You're Not Normal is the three-word cortisol death sentence to recovery, Me Too is the two-word pardon you get at group self-help meetings. The mask we think we had to wear anywhere else in public can—thankfully—be left at the door.

Even if you do not ever buy into the 12 steps as a design for living, they are *suggested*, not required, for membership. "The only requirement is a desire to stop drinking," the literature says. Twelve-step meetings are places to be among others who feel the same, wore the same masks, suffer the same Symptoms and have a desire to communicate rather than drink over them. "The most desperate need of mankind today is not a new vaccine for any disease or a new religion or a new way of life," wrote Taylor Caldwell in the novel *The Listener*. (Bantam Books, New York 1984) "His real need, his most terrible need, is for someone to listen to him, not as a patient but as a human soul."

Everyone, no matter how gifted, healthy or wealthy, encounters an issue that baffles them or breaks the spirit. Self-help groups are where we can communicate the baffling and the spirit-breaking. What we're all trying to do together is acquire back our self-esteem. Assertiveness is for when people don't give it back willingly or compassionately . . . and the self-help group is for making sure self-doubt or guilt or shame don't pry it from us again.

Look at these words: Brave, clever, intelligent, resourceful, right, moral, trustworthy, praiseworthy, emotionally strong, physically strong. You can be a *modest* Alcoholic and still describe yourself with those qualities. If you haven't used any of these to describe yourself in the last month, the stressors and the cortisol are winning. There's a group meeting somewhere near you in about an hour that can help you begin to repair your compromised self-esteem. How was your self-esteem before Alcoholism? Mine was healthy. Not obnoxiously or perpetually self-confident, just proudly capable. I lost that. Communicating in a group got that back for me. I might not ever use those words above to describe me all at once, but the meetings and the communication brought back a few.

I'm no shill for AA. The slogan factory drives me nuts. More about this in a moment. I hate the coffee. The Higher Power thing is tough for some people to swallow. Some people stay away from 12-step meetings because they don't see themselves in the people around the tables or hear their stories told in the tragic stories of others. That is the point in going: To make sure you're communicating what is stressing you before you go back to the drinking and *become* those tragic stories. You go because you don't want to become The Alcoholic You Don't Want To Be.

I screwed that one up, big time. When I first went to a 12-step meeting, I was Alcoholic. No Doubt About It. But I didn't hear myself *as I presently was* in the stories. I heard the horror stories. I was a functioning, maintenance drinker with a great job, two cars, etc. I didn't have this low bottom I heard in the other stories. So I walked away, not realizing that *that day* could have been my bottom. Their stories of grief and shame weren't *me*. I had great empathy for their ordeals. What I failed to see was that they were a gift, showing me where I was headed, not where I was. That these ordeals of theirs were mine if I didn't make that day my bottom. They were the Alcoholics I Didn't Want To Be. At the dawn of AA in the 1930s, the makeup was men and women with low, low bottoms. Over the years, that changed mainly because those who had hit low bottoms were able to raise the bottom to a level where it applies to Alcoholics-in-training like me who hadn't had a low bottom. Yet. I failed. I didn't listen . . . there's that communication thing again . . . to what they were saying that they, too, were one day in the same shape I was. And then I became the Alcoholic I Didn't Want To Be a few years down the road. While we have to talk about the stuff we don't talk about, it pays to listen. A lot.

From a strictly medical standpoint, Alcoholism is remarkably easy to arrest. It's a lot less complicated than arresting cancer or diabetes. We abandon the bottle long enough and detox and biological functioning returns to something close to normal in a few weeks or months. From that point on, it is a matter of not going backward. "That's the drawback to having a disease that can be arrested but not cured," say Rogers and McMillin. "While it is under control it's all too easy to forget what life was like when it wasn't." Self-help groups remind us of that, which is another benefit of 12-step meetings beyond people-providing.

Too much people-providing can be bad, some opponents of group therapy and group self-help claim. They make a really valid point in becoming over reliant on the group. Addiction to meetings is potentially as destructive to the family as is our addiction to alcohol. It's like when Hawaii had a rat problem, they imported mongooses from Asia. They killed the rats. And the dogs. And the cats, children and small pigs. They traded a rat problem for a mongoose problem.

A common theme heard at both group therapy and group self-help is frustration. When you feel this, it is an undeniable sign that you *are* moving forward toward recovery. Whitfield says a key to getting free of frustration is tolerating it long enough to explore it and work through it *out loud* and with others. "In the past, some of us may have run away [from frustration] or beat ourselves up over it. It is in the safety and support of a group that we can learn to tolerate emotional pain more clearly and successfully, work through conflict and grow from it."

Acceptance of your whole self is a goal of recovery. Accepting the disease, accepting what you did or didn't do, accepting that you're changed permanently, accepting the labeling that inevitably will continue. All are part of accepting your whole self and communicating in a group helps you see that acceptance is okay. Are you using others to achieve this goal? You bet you are. They are, too. It's called a *support* group, remember. You are giving back. Just by being there.

One of the most treasured AA stories in print says, "Above all, AA taught me how to handle sobriety. I have learned how to relate to people . . . deal with disappointments and problems that once would have sent me right to the bottle. How do we do it? By sharing at meetings." Twelve-step meetings help prevent you from taking your stressors too far, to the point of self-pity. And drinking.

I am not by temperament or training an optimist. The pithy one-day-at-a-time mantras and other optimistic syrup oozing out of the AA slogan factory, taken by themselves, turn me off. But I keep coming back because the meetings work as a safe venue for communicating my frustrations and stressors and talking about my Symptoms. I'm pragmatic and cautious and suspicious of everyone's motives. Even my own are not exempt. So it is hard for me to go to meetings at times. I find no substitute for the proven people-providing effectiveness of AA and the safety I find in its meetings, so I go.

Some people say it makes them happy to go to a 12-step meeting. Not me. It is a relief, not a happiness. It's what it takes for me to live with myself, live with my guilt and live with others, not what makes me happy. "I don't think happiness or unhappiness is the point," says Bill Wilson. (*As Bill Sees It*, AA World Services, New York 1967) "How do we meet the problems we face? How do we best learn from them and transmit what we have learned to others if they would receive the knowledge?"

Dozens of research studies indicate going to AA meetings *regularly* is the greatest predictor of a stable, long-term recovery. Many AA alternatives spend a lot of energy being anti-12-step instead of pro-recovery. They are not as easy to find either. Several I found knocked AA, not in their literature but in the talk at the tables. They knock AA at their own peril. It is the rescue of first resort to many people, but it is a very accessible and open-24-hours solace of last resort when you're staring down a lapse. For some of us, it is the last house on the block.

The task of sober living is daunting. It is like fighting terrorism: You have to be right 100 percent of the time. To be perceived as a failure, an attacker needs only to succeed once. To "fail" in sobriety by public standards, alcohol needs only to pass your lips once. The great advantage among the many offered by support groups is that around their tables lapse is not condemned. You are among men and women who understand how daunting the task is. Which brings me to another point: All meetings have personalities.

Because there are so many self-help groups, you can shop around. I found one that mostly matches my personality, gender and background. The communication is easier. The common ground you have in any group has to be more than just the disease, because we all have different factors in our lives that affect our recoveries. Finding the right environment, the right group, is the number one factor of success in sobriety.

Chapter Ten

Schlimmbesserung—noun/German/: A fix that makes things worse.

WARNING: Some of the next 12 paragraphs are offensive (they were for me to write them let alone live them) and they are socially indelicate.

There's a 19-year-old gangsta/armed robber—also calls himself a "street ni___." Pretty much hourly. His name is Mac. He named himself that though... which has something to do with how much of a smooth playah he is with the females. Oh, and he raps, too, and Mac is easier to put into rhyme than Jacquaris.

We began a second week together with him showing up late, not bothering with a shirt and his pants hanging off his butt, yelling, "Hey my ni___," to his pal less than five feet away. I don't care that he and I don't speak much, lest I become "his ni___," too.

It doesn't get any better this week.

We did not speak for almost three days after he openly mocked my plan to stay sober and I retorted that he wouldn't see my age unless someone locked him up. He gave me that street-punk waggish laugh like he's just heard the funniest joke ever. And that was where things stood for 72 hours.

When we were on speaking terms, I didn't actually comprehend many of the words, sounds and concepts other than that I was part of some "white ass booshit" conspiracy, that his girlfriend was a "ho," and that we have to "keep it real, fam" if we were going to "peaceibbly coexist." His "ho," by the way was Dezarray. Not to be confused with his "bitch," Shawna, who is also the "babymomma" for their four-year-old. Did I mention he is 19? Mac and

Shawna have a child because she angered him once by going out to the clubs and his revenge was to "put a baby in her."

Mac charmed me with three stories. We *have* to spend time together in our group so I have no choice but to hear this dark triad. One's about pimping women out, one's about ripping off cell phones and "slappin' da shit out of Shawna," the third's about the day he "got popped" (arrested).

The first story: Apparently I, too, can be a pimp. Mac believes I can. "Girls don't want to sell dope. They want to sell p___." He says I'd be surprised to find out how many do, even the "fine-ass bitches." When you pimp, he claims, the girls give you all the money. They just want you to buy them stuff. With their money. And give them a place to stay. And have their backs. I can trick them out on chat lines and send them out, he says. And here I thought college was the way to achieve my dreams. Mac sometimes sends them out with a bottle so they can get the date drunk and rob him when he passes out. Other times he just follows her and robs the guy himself. A guy like me smells like money according to Mac and that should make it easy for me to get girls to trick for me, their pimp. Smelling like money is how Mac got Dezarray after all.

They met at a party and she *needed* him to pimp her out. So he sneaked her out of the party to the store on the corner so he could buy cigarillos and so he could park her on a bus stop. Within 20 minutes she was gone in a pickup truck. In an hour she gave Mac the money and a bag of chips she bought at the store when she was dropped off.

Retelling that story to me got Mac all sentimental about Shawna. Hasn't pimped her out yet. Because she is mentally disabled and he doesn't need her to do that because she gives him her Social Security disability check.

Which brings me to story two. Shawna is good with stealing cell phones. Do you really have to steal them these days? Mobile companies practically give them away. But the pay part of pay-as-you-go wireless plans is the part Mac doesn't like and he has Shawna steal them. At the mall, on buses. Just snatch them and use them until the service gets shut off, which usually takes a while because who carries a second phone on them just in case you have to call in the theft of the first? Shawna found out Mac was using the phones she'd procure for him to call other girls and she confronted him. So he punched her, then choked the same neck upon which she had his name tattooed.

Story three. Mac was rolling through the 'hood on Milwaukee's north side, "high as a bitch with my n___s," he reports. Had the stereo "bumpin' in the Monte (Carlo)." They were looking for a gang banger who took a swing at Mac the day before, the sub-woofer announcing their presence a block away. But the bumpin' wasn't so loud that they didn't hear the shots their mark was now firing at the car. They fled to Kenosha to get some weaponry of their own from a guy Mac sold some heroin to earlier.

Mac's a little parched doing all the story telling, so he takes a swig of Kool-Aid he made with Mountain Dew instead of water. Don't worry about the sugar's impact on his dental work: It's gold.

In Kenosha, Mac grabbed a sawed-off shotgun from the addict, then turned it on the doper to steal his money, and went back to the Monte and his friends waiting curbside down the block. With a squad car parked behind them. The Milwaukee gunfire drew attention to the car. Mac tossed the sawed-off shotgun into the bushes and took off on foot for 17 blocks before being caught.

Repulsed by those 12 paragraphs?
Try getting well next to such a distraction.

Story three is how Jacquaris and I ended up in the same one-size-fits-all alcohol and drug group therapy. I drank and drove, he was a drug dealer who fudged the assessment to get into the program and get a shorter sentence. His story isn't even the worst, only the most printable. There are sociologists and social workers who, as a vocal minority, believe in social experiments like putting Mac and me together because of the diversity and how we can learn from our differences. This is recovery, not the United Nations or some Coca-Cola commercial. There's a lot at stake in our recoveries to be playing around with cultural experiments. I believe in maximizing the probability of success, and no one did Mac or me any favors in that department. Mac's distraction doesn't guarantee my failure in the group. It does nothing to guarantee success, though. When people share as little common ground as he and I did, communication fails. We didn't even speak the same language most days.

I may have lapped from some dirty puddles in my darkest times but nothing on my bib matches this stain. I just wanted to resume my three-and-a-half year recovery and instead I got pimp lessons.

I needed to hear my voice in his stories, I needed him to hear his voice in mine. I don't relate well to Garrison Keillor-type tales either and didn't expect them.

I did *not* expect a distraction on the level of Mac's depravity though. I believe every life, even his, has value, but not all lives have value to recovery though.

That's not recovery snobbery or elitism in thinking he has no business in my recovery: I have no illusion that I am good for *his* recovery either (if he wanted one—more on motivation in a moment). My stories were as foreign to him as French. He has a right to treatment if that's what he wants. The point is we are all equal, but we are not the same. The environment of our group was ignored when Mac and I were put with each other (a.k.a. ordered). He wasn't going to ask for another group over it because all he had to do was fake it for six months so he could get out early and go back to selling dope. I wasn't going to ask for another group because if I requested it, I'd face 18 more months of jail myself. The environment failed us. Neither of us learned much of anything of relapse prevention because of the noisy distraction of our differences in age, culture, education, etc.

My cortisol was unchanged. Maybe even worse. I lost 40 lbs. Didn't communicate through my shame or guilt or grief. I got a certificate. And I was sent out the door needing more therapy than I needed coming in it. I don't bring up the ordeal for the "poor me" play: It's poor *you*. You paid for both of us.

Mac proves two points. One point, which I made in my previous book, is that this sort of hustler bluffs his way into programs not so he can get better but so he can get away from consequences for his behavior and get back to victimizing the planet. The second point is that when certain success characteristics are ignored they become barriers to communication and recovery in group therapy/group self-help.

Several success characteristics create the environment for moving toward recovery. According to Cloud and Granfield, they are well-known but easily, and often, overlooked. "Although psychologists and social workers may have undergone professional training that underscores the critical role that gender, class and other socio-demographic characteristics play in creating and sustaining dysfunctional alcohol use, much of this perspective is ignored in the actual treatment of dysfunctional alcohol use."

Here are the success characteristics for group therapy and group self-help, in priority order, they are: Level of Motivation; Type of Drug and Severity of Use; and, Demographics. The more of them you can match among a majority of the participants in the groups you are looking at joining, the better the probability of avoiding lapse. The emphasis is not on *all* characteristics for *all* participants. That would mean you are trying to "compare out" of a certain group or meeting. This is about identifying—seeing how much you're like others—rather than looking for ways you are different.

Success Characteristic One: Level of Motivation

Do you want to be there and how badly?

It has taken treatment professionals decades to find The Source of motivation for treatment and relapse prevention. They want to know what button to push to get someone into treatment. And it is really pretty basic: You have a fatal disease and a toxic chemical is shortening your life but you can survive it if you want. A person who believes this has motivation for recovery and will strive for it, according to Rogers and McMillin. "If you don't believe it, then you won't [have motivation]. As crisis passes and pressure eases, all other motivation seems to drain away like fuel from a leaking tank. Relapse will follow." If you're not in trouble, and you don't realize how fatal the disease is (Chapter Eleven), drinking is such a part of our culture that you can go back to it easily.

Thugs and conwomen who do not have motivation will bring the group down. The more you can avoid them and associate with those who get it that this disease is fatal, the better the chances for success. Unfortunately, much of the treatment delivery system today is focused on headcounts, not outcomes, thanks to the legal system and health insurance contracts. It is focused on compliance, and you will find in every group someone who is in there to save their job, their marriage or their freedom. That doesn't make them automatically bad for your recovery. Many of them understand the disease and genuinely want to be there to save their own lives.

You cannot ignore the fact that if someone does not desire to get better they won't get better.

Motivation is not a challenge unique to alcohol treatment. Take, for example, how motivational difficulties can interfere with cardiac patients. Told to change their diets, they just aren't interested in ditching the cheeseburger and fries. They don't see the connection between death and what they are putting into their bodies. National Council on Alcoholism and Drug Dependence (NCADD) pioneer Ross von Wiegand noted, "The single most important aspect of a successful recovery from Alcoholism is motivation to accept treatment." In the case of group therapy or group self-help, if the guy next to you isn't motivated, it can impact you.

"For nearly all there is some degree of ambivalence at the outset," adds Cloud, who also ranks the characteristic highly. "The importance of wishing to alter one's relationship with substances cannot be overstated." Coerced group programs have low success rates thanks to this seemingly basic prerequisite. There are a lot of people conning the system by BSing the assessments and/or unskilled assessors to have the spot next to you in group. They come in all stripes, but their goal has nothing to do with the motivation to avoid death but to avoid immediate consequence. They talk the talk to get in, but they are not there to fit in. They sound eager for treatment. They are eager to stay out of the pokey or the unemployment line or divorce court.

You can't be skeptical of everyone. Their program isn't yours to run. But yours is yours to run. Don't let those who don't share your motivation tear down your sobriety though. To their ends, they will not be able to keep saying the right things to the right people all the time and they will fail at groups. Someone will smell them out or they'll compare themselves out, but in the meantime they can do a lot of damage trying to bring others to the brink with them by holding on to their old ideas. Despite well-scripted motivation claims, they are using groups as a part of a hidden agenda to drink again or slip past consequences if they do get a buzz on again. They don't see death as a major consequence. It's not their motivation to communicate *with* the group but to communicate *to* the group and you are their victim. Treatment or support groups are their damage control. Nothing more.

Some instincts we all share, like wanting to escape stressors or pain, such as the Symptoms. Some instincts are the province of con artists, and they seek self-preservation only, not giving a damn about the communication we need as Alcoholics. Those latter instincts translate into escape *from* group, the rest of us escape *to* group. Without exception, Alcoholics on the fence between escaping from the group and drinking or going to a group meeting have no regrets going to group therapy or a group self-help meeting . . . if they have motivation. It is easier to drink than going to a meeting. If a person is firmly not in touch with the finality of this disease, they will go to the drink if there isn't a strong person next to him that shares the motivation to stay away. Call it a sponsor, or a mentor, or a friend . . . you're not going to get through sobriety without a similarly motivated human being in the chair next to you.

A flaw in the public treatment delivery system today is that you cannot find a program or self-help group without some participants there by force. You'll find few private treatment facilities who do not make an effort to screen out those ordered into treatment without any other motivation because they are disruptive to paying patients and sack success rate statistics. That's the cold-hard fact of private delivery of services in a competitive environment: They don't have to accept everyone and they'll only accept people with motivation because the unmotivated—the ones who don't see finality—equal lapse and they screw up brochures touting how good the facility is. The lesson we can all learn from that capitalistic view is that if the Alcoholic next to you doesn't want to be there, it diminishes your chances.

Motivation is not an all-or-nothing proposition. Some groupers *are* motivated by saving the job or marriage or freedom. Maybe someone did force them into the group. Yet, after the initial motivation in things like the job or the marriage they realized that if they lost the job or the wife, they're still on a path leading to the center of that chart: Death. So do not be quick to judge those in your group by force. Many do come around. Just know that if you have a group of spectacularly unmotivated men and women, your chances of success drop like a stone.

We all know the characters of Dorothy, Tin Man, Lion and Scarecrow from L. Frank Baum's 1900 *Wizard of Oz*. The story is a metaphor for how groups can succeed when the ONLY characteristic the group shares is motivation. The characters were all different, very different. But they shared motivation and that alone allowed each character to learn from each other and lean on each other to get what they sought individually. They gave up struggles with themselves and became involved with each other and succeeded. If *one* wasn't motivated, the group would have failed.

Even the Wizard got something out of witnessing the motivation of *the group*: Humility. "I'm really a very good man, though I am a very bad wizard I must admit."

Success Characteristic Two: Type of drug/severity of use

There are many in the treatment business who would have you believe a drug addict and Alcoholic and alcohol abuser are so close they should be sharing a kidney if not sharing the same program. Not true.

Alcoholics and alcohol abusers are different even though the same chemical is associated with both and even if the two conditions are often lumped together for reasons of mistake, laziness or budget. A whiskey Alcoholic, a wine Alcoholic and a beer Alcoholic are more alike than a whiskey alcohol abuser, a wine abuser and a beer abuser. All six of the above, while different, share more in common with each other than they do with crackheads, potheads or tweakers (meth addicts). Yes, we're all struggling. But it isn't the same. In the case of public programs, someone needs to do an assessment to see which group you fit . . . often a lax process as I pointed out in *What the Early Worm Gets*. In the case of group self-help, you have to make that call.

Alcohol is not the same as other chemicals and Alcoholism is not the same as other problems. Insurers, public policy makers and more than a fair share of people who've never been challenged by chemicals would have you believe we are identical. We're worlds apart actually. Drugging starts with a conscious, deliberate, illegal act: The choice to buy a substance which is not legal to buy. To get yourself there, you knowingly decide to go to That Part of Town, not to aisle ten in the supermarket where you easily find the booze. Drugging is a different mindset, a different set of risks, than Alcohol Use Disorders. For that connection to a sub-culture alone, drug abusers and alcohol use disorders demand to be managed separately. No program can address both and succeed at either. If your group proposes to do that, think about alternatives.

Marijuana is only psychologically addictive, not physically. Heroin is a street drug unavailable the way alcohol is. Oxycodone is a prescription drug, dissimilar to alcohol and pot and weed. Inhalant abusers and tweakers and crackheads are all as uniquely different from one another as their drugs of choice. What you use, how long you use it, and your level of involvement with the subculture or criminal activity are all factors impacting how we communicate to each other.

Let's look at Mac again. Not properly assessed for drug of choice, involvement with sub-culture or motivation . . . he and I should never have crossed paths. We may have been the result of ignoble mandates and naïve courts/legislatures, but we existed in each other's worlds. I disrupted his group recovery. He disrupted mine. I screwed recovery up for him if that's what he wanted, he certainly distracted mine.

Many drug users are, in fact, more criminal and people with antisocial personality disorders are a poor fit with those who don't have a history of drug-sub-culture thinking. There's a simple 12-question test most skilled counselors administer upon intake. It's easy to get offended by the questions if you take it as an accusation or assumption that a counselor believes you are a sociopath. The test is actually a filter to help you into a group more suitable to your recovery needs based on success characteristic two. It comes in two parts:

Part 1: BEFORE AGE 15

1. Skipped school. I often skipped school because I didn't want to be there or because I wanted to do other things.
2. Ran away. I ran away at least two times overnight.
3. Fights. I started or participated in physical fights more than once.
4. Weapons. I used a gun, knife, club or other weapon more than once.
5. Sex. I forced someone into sexual activity.
6. Cruelty to animals. I hurt animals intentionally.
7. Cruelty to people. I hurt people intentionally.
8. Property damage. I destroyed or damaged other people's property on purpose.
9. Fires. I set fires on purpose.
10. Lying. I lied frequently.
11. Theft. I took things that didn't belong to me, or forged checks, broke into places, used others' identities or online accounts more than once.
12. Robbery. I forced people to give me the things that belonged to them.

PART TWO: SINCE AGE 15

13. Work problems. I haven't worked when work was available, have skipped work or college classes because I wanted to, or have quit several jobs or schools without any future plans.
14. Illegal activities. I have committed crimes and done illegal things for which I could have been arrested.
15. Violence. I have had physical fights.
16. Irresponsibility. I have failed to pay child support, bills or take care of my family.
17. Moving around. I have moved without having a job, drifted from place to place or lived without a home for more than a month at a time.
18. Conning. I have lied, used false names or hustled people to get what I wanted.
19. Reckless. I have driven a car recklessly or have acted in ways that caused danger to others.
20. Parenting. I have not taken care of my children by leaving them alone, not feeding them or depending on others to take care of them for me.
21. Relationships. I have never been able to stay faithful to a lover for more than a year.
22. Remorse. I don't feel bad most of the time when I steal from, hurt or treat someone else badly.

Add up the yesses in Part One. If you have three or more yes answers, you have a habit of using antisocial behavior that started early in life and will probably be difficult to change. Add up the yesses in Part Two. If you have four or more yes answers you have a history of continuing antisocial behavior as an adult.

This diagnostic tool is from the Diagnostic and Statistical Manual of Mental Disorders (DSM), the blue book for professionals working in the mental health field. Internationally recognized recovery and relapse expert Gorski reads the DSM questionnaire results this way when applying them to alcohol use disorders: "If you did not have three or more yes answers in Part One it may mean your behavior is completely connected to alcohol use. One way to make sure is to review your yes answers in Part Two and ask yourself if these things always happened when you were trying to get alcohol, using alcohol or because you had been using alcohol recently." (*Relapse Prevention Therapy*, Herald House/Independence Books, Independence, MO 1993) A person who is antisocial *without* the alcohol is not the same as someone who is antisocial only with the alcohol. Success characteristic two depends upon treating the two separately and specifically. There's a whole different set of gears driving the antisocial drug user.

Success Characteristic Three: Demographics

We are all equal. We are not all the same. Ethnicity, gender, education, employment and age are census fields and traits helpful in determining group success and successful communication. We have to—*have to*—have humility in recovery. But who said that means abandoning common sense like healing alongside people most like you? Alcoholism observes no boundaries at age or gender or social status, but recovery does tend to be more successful when such traits are observed as boundaries.

When it comes to treatment or self-help we have to stop with the hypersensitivity to political correctness that otherwise dictates how Americans handle anything that could approach treating someone separately by age, culture or gender. Do you want the group to work or do you want it to be politically correct? Do we get a badge for this? The abject, brute reality is that separation works.

I'm not advocating intolerance nor am I citing any clinician who thinks that is a good idea. Acknowledging our differences and respecting that we heal faster around those with whom we have things we share in common flies in the face of diversity. Sometimes diversity dilutes results. If I have one admonishment in these pages it is this: Do not ever use this as an excuse out of a group. None of us is so terminally unique that no group measures up. This is the last of the three success characteristics, the final sort, not the first or only.

It pays not to judge on demographic criteria. Among the people I learned most from . . . one is female, one is African-American. The point of considering demographics at all has nothing to do with how much the rest of the group looks but how our biology and culture shapes priorities in life and recovery.

For example, gender matters if you prefer same-sex meetings, but it also matters because physiologically women suffer more damage and quicker than men do, plus they are stereotypically more susceptible to guilt. To their credit they are far less chickenshit to talk about it openly either. That makes some of my Y-chromosome counterparts uncomfortable, but I find it is a benefit rather than a drawback.

Alfred Kinsey's 1948 *Sexual Behavior in the Human Male* (W. B. Saunders Company, New York) is known worldwide as the most thorough study of its kind ever, but it also contains a most powerful statement on human diversity and the importance of overlapping experiences. "The world is not to be divided into sheep and goats. Not all things are black nor all things white. It is a fundamental of taxonomy that nature rarely deals with discrete categories. Only the human mind invents categories and tries to force facts into separate pigeonholes. The living world is a continuum in each and every aspect." It is not being the sheep color or the sheep shape, it's living the sheep experience and if the rest of the group aren't sheep your chance for success dimishes. Variation and uniqueness are the norm among individuals in group experiences, but it is among the shared gender experiences that we get past sobriety.

Age matters, too, because of communication challenges over generations and maturity. In my case and in eight of ten people I interviewed, a 40-something man in recovery prefers to be around guys who think it is "Gucci" to have *quit* drinking two liters a day instead of guys who thought it was Gucci to have been able to drink that much and the younger guys didn't prefer to be around guys they had to explain Gucci to.

Ethnicity or culture is a demographic factor. Don't pretend to be offended: You *know* it matters and that culture is a major determinant of anyone's values, beliefs, behaviors and communication.

So are education and employment. I'll tell this much, I'd rather have as a group the loggers I've met versus the mutual fund industry managers with whom I have worked. Employment matters not for what you do but for the availability a person has for regular group attendance. And some people may have lost work due to alcohol: Someone still clinging to a job or has never had the boss question them is not going to relate to that pain. Education level has to do with the flow of the conversation and, for group therapy, how complex the treatment gets. Several Alcoholics have given me stories of how counselors use education and employment to make their group more diverse. They claim it is a teaching tool. I found myself in not one, but two programs—one intensive outpatient and one six-month residential—where the counselor insisted upon keeping me in a group that didn't want me there because of my education and employment background. They voiced the concern repeatedly that I wasn't like them. But I was the teaching tool and an example for them. I wasn't there to prove her points or be an example for anyone. I sure didn't want to be excluded, either, by a bunch of men who were just as broken as I but who believed I was somehow less than them because I don't swing a hammer. I needed to belong. I just wanted to stay sober.

Cloud adds additional personal attributes to the success characteristic: Family status, health, hobbies, religion. All aid in communication because they expand the common ground upon which we walk. A point made as long ago as the 1971 Report to Congress on Alcohol and Health (the first-ever by the National Institute on Alcoholism and Alcohol Abuse) was that, "To be successful, treatment must consider the body and its chemistry. So also must love, hate and fear that reside in the unconscious level of our minds, within our roles in social groups. Alcoholism is a complicated disease, but it can be treated successfully. Any technique used indiscrimately will be much less successful. When proper treatment modalities reflect the unique needs of the patient, however, we indeed have a cause for optimism."

Don't underestimate the value of getting help *before* you're coerced into it because if you're forced in, you will have little if any ability to shop for a group meeting your own communication needs. This point also emphasizes the role of community and of criminal justice to better assess people entering programs and to organize them, as much as budget permits. Without proper and thorough assessment the money isn't particularly well targeted and the programs are less effective.

No two of us are driven by the same desires, the same rages, the same thoughts, impulses, responsibilities or the same nerve. All Alcoholics share the same bad biochemistry and flawed genes, but unless our demographics overlap, this just isn't enough common ground. Success characteristic three helps close the gap.

The more of the success characteristics we share, the better we communicate and avoid lapse. All that stuff we don't talk about but need to talk about is going to come out easier when you are with people most like you. Empathy only carries you so far.

I truly don't know the first thing about how an alcohol abuser deals with forgiveness, but I know a lot about how Alcoholics struggle with it. I don't know squat about what Arab-Americans are challenged with, or the guilt of Mexican-Americans may feel for families a border away. I'm highly sensitive to women's issues having been raised well by two . . . but I'm really inadequate in helping mom's talk about grief that comes with the end of childbearing years. Most men guess and we're usually way off. A laborer who works harder than I do or ever did isn't going to get a whole lot of wisdom from my corner-office ups and downs. A younger man with healthy parents isn't going to have the sense of urgency about forgiveness that I have as a son with only one parent left who just might not be here long enough for all the apologies that need to be spoken. An experienced parent would help me see it is a thousand times more important to celebrate my kids at their ages today, not beat myself up for the ages lost, the First Communion dress I didn't see on my princess or the bleacher dad/philosopher I couldn't be. Mac is going to help me with this?

What I do know is how much it helps when other people relate to exactly what I experience because they had the same experience. Emotions I thought were deeper were just under the surface when I had those familiar people by my side in group. Sadness, exhaustion, worry and stress mean the same thing to people who are alike. The thick skin I sometimes wear and the tears I often cry aren't known by people as dissimilar to me as a Mac. "Why can't I find work?" isn't a question he grapples with. I went from complete pro to unemployable because of my record, he went from loser to hero because of his. My skills never diminished, his never were developed. I was shamed out of Prudential and Circle K convenience store jobs, he held them up. Regardless of the pinnacles either of us reached in our lives, we haven't eyed the same ones. The Tin Man was stuck with Tupac.

Can a boy who had a child to spite his girlfriend come to the table with the perspective of a kind and gentle dad to help me see how irrational my guilt is? He was more impressed that I drank two liters a day than that I stopped drinking two liters a day. Can a pimp who's never worked a day in his life comprehend the mourning with which I struggled at the disintegration of my career? When recovery fails, it isn't the easy access to beer or the lack of willpower, it is the presence of the Macs in our lives when we really need someone to relate to so we can belong.

How do you communicate the grief over losing respect if you are talking with someone who never had any?

The story I shared about the Loneliest Place in America back in chapter three, might as well have been in French.

An Alcoholic lives in two worlds and fits in neither. He's ostracized himself from the primary world—the one that judges him "not normal"—and the one he's jammed into with Macs that is completely alien, stereotyped and uncomfortable. When we are among others that speak the same language, feel the same feelings and communicate the same way, we find our way back to a primary world that welcomes us.

People lapse when they get stuck with Mac and don't communicate through the grief, guilt, shame and forgiveness issues. So it pays to shop for your group. The success characteristics support communication. The Symptoms thrive on not meeting the success characteristics.

For me, I went into my second rehab needing relapse prevention tactics and someone to talk to. I came out needing more help than when I went in. Schlimmbesserung. My needs were unmet and worsened. I have 100 percent responsibility for meeting them when I can deliver on shopping for my group based on the three success characteristics.

Mac, by the way, won't be reading this. Not as a free man anyway. He is behind bars. Sexual assault. I apparently wasn't really good for his recovery either. So much for diversity and being an example.

Chapter Eleven

"When a lot of remedies are suggested for a disease that means it can't be cured."—Anton Chekov, "The Cherry Orchard"

What I mean by needing more help was that I not only still had the lapse and communication problems, I now had a self-esteem problem after that foul group environment. There's a counter-productive notion that Alcoholics need their self-esteem ridiculously battered to make them better. It's popular to believe we should be met with brutal humiliation. I attempted to research the source of this practice and came up with no credible foundation for it. It's just the way the stigma plays itself out in treatment.

A bad group peeled back my self-image to new lows in the name of rehabilitating me while at the same time I'm learning from every reputable alcohologist that no Alcoholic EVER is rehabilitated for long without a healthy sense of self-worth. I wanted mine back. And I got it. Apparently after nearing suicide and surviving Mac's atmosphere I have more shock absorber in me than I believed. However, my recovery didn't make progress until I was permitted to join a group of my choosing.

Let's face it, I wasn't a hostage in Syria. A bad group is punishing but it isn't a brutal physical ordeal. I am no victim. Many people have endured real tragedies for longer. The detour I was on was survivable. I was trapped, forced to accept as okay deviant behavior I do not and have not ever accepted as okay. Finding a group that met the success criteria righted a lot of wrongs. Being free to communicate mended the corrosion.

It's a personal victory, one I care about. It's also a more universal victory that everyone can care about because every day any Alcoholic is not drinking over failed treatment, no treatment or the Symptoms of Sobriety is a day with less drain on the healthcare system. The stress relieved from the economy and culture by successful management of the disease is real and measurable. Our society tends to dismiss the risks and downplay the hazards of alcohol use. Bud Light commercials and Captain Morgan girls have skillfully illustrated their vision of what alcohol does *for* you but left out what it does *to* you.

Here's the rest of the story, unspun by special interests.

Alcohol is a mass killer in the United States and is the defining public health issue for the 21st century. Driving under the influence has statistically little to do with that conclusion.

Eleven thousand motor vehicle deaths, 40 percent of the total, stem from alcohol-related crashes. To put that into context with other preventable deaths:

157,000 lung cancer deaths annually
50,000 people are killed in gun violence
39,520 breast cancer deaths
37,000 fatal overdoses from prescription drugs
34,000 suicides
30,000 Americans still die of the *flu*
18,000 people are killed in our hospitals by staph infections

Every alcohol-related car crash death is heartbreaking, but by the numbers, those deaths make up very little of the death toll from alcohol use. Even if you ended drinking and driving, alcohol is still our nation's number one killer.
89,000 other deaths (not in cars) are directly attributed to alcohol
1,000,000 more fatalities from diseases are indirectly attributed to alcohol (e.g. alcohol causes a condition leading to death)

It's easy to be offended by drinking and driving. What's even more offensive is the underreporting of the health effects of alcohol that prove alcohol is our defining health issue. Tobacco has at times held that mantle, but by comparison, only 473,000 die annually of smoking-related illness. Beverage alcohol kills more than a million. A 2012 study by the German University Medicine Greifswald found that heavy drinkers are at *more risk* of death than those who smoke. (Ulrich John, Hans-Jürgen Rumpf in *Alcoholism: Clinical and Experimental Research*, November 2012)

The way America has responded to tobacco awareness campaigns holds promise for alcohol awareness campaigns, should one be mounted. In 1967, smoking was "in." Seventy-six percent of adult men smoked. Today smoking is "out" and health officials at the Food and Drug Administration believe by 2020 smoking will be banned in all states. This is happening within just a generation and a half because smoking's health effects are no longer underreported or reported only in obscure medical publications. With alcohol as with smoking, people are entitled to their own opinions, but they are not entitled to their own facts on the health consequences. We haven't been given them.

About eight percent of the population is Alcoholic and 35 percent are alcohol abusers, but in a November 18, 2011 ABC News/Gallup Poll, 67 percent of Americans admitted to having ever abused alcohol. The CDC puts the number at 61.2 percent currently drinking frequently and 14 percent former regular drinkers. Those numbers nearly mirror the smoking stats from 1967 before people began learning of the health toll of tobacco.

Here are the direct and indirect health risks for anyone who uses alcohol. The risks apply to light to moderate drinkers, not just a hard drinker. They call for more and better treatment for alcohol use disorders, because if we're not treating them or aggressively managing Symptoms of Sobriety, we're spending more than $221 billion caring for alcohol-related hospitalizations and diseases. The following statistics are released drip by drip in various reports each year, but when taken together, they are quite damning. The direct impacts of alcohol are associated with getting drunk, being drunk or activity while drunk. The indirect impacts can surface even years after alcohol use due to the toxicity of alcohol to healthy tissues.

Note: I'll cite the sources only for material not coming from CDC or NIH resources.

Direct health consequences

Four percent of deaths globally are linked directly to alcohol according to the University of Toronto Centre for Addiction & Mental Health 2009 study. One in ten deaths in Europe outpaces our own 5.5 percent . . . one in 10,000 in the eastern Mediterranean is the lowest. The most common categories for *direct* causes of death documented include the following.

Alcohol Poisoning

The first symptom most people experience is sudden death. There is no way of accurately gauging how close you are to a lethal dose of alcohol until you pass it.

Tolerance Dose vs. Lethal Dose

[Chart: BAC vs. Time showing curves for Lethal dose, Alcoholic pass out dose, Alcoholic buzz dose, Non-Alcoholic pass out dose, and Non-Alcoholic buzz dose. Annotation: "Alcoholics have a very narrow gap between lethal dose and pass out dose." Points A and B marked on chart.]

Ⓐ Following a pattern of heavy drinking, an Alcoholic's buzz dose can actually drop

Ⓑ Without predictability, an Alcoholic's buzz dose can spike well past lethal levels. He can pass out and die without feeling a buzz at all.

College students have passed out and OD'd on lower levels than I've been caught at behind the wheel. Singer Amy Winehouse died in 2011 at a BAC five times higher than the legal limit for driving but twice before had been hospitalized at higher BAC levels. You just don't know when you are not going to wake up.

Withdrawal

Absence of alcohol can and does kill Alcoholics because the disease quickly alters the body's tissues. They become dependent upon alcohol, *requiring* it in the bloodstream constantly or the body begins to shut down during withdrawal, much as it would without oxygen. Alcohol withdrawal is the only drug withdrawal that can be fatal. Not heroin or meth, the alcohol you find in aisle six of the Winn-Dixie. Heroin addicts may wish for death during withdrawal but won't actually die from it.

Researchers Glen Hanson, Peter Venturelli and Annette Fleckenstein (*Drugs and Society*, Bartlett Publishers, Sudbury, MA 2009) found "About five percent of Alcoholics in hospitals and perhaps 20-25 without treatment during withdrawal die" suffering from delirium tremens (DTs—high fever, heartbeat irregularities, etc.). Basically, an Alcoholic can die for a drink. Medically supervised detoxification is a need for Alcoholics because of life support, not for the sedatives to make the other pains of withdrawal more bearable. The most accurate I can be in describing my own withdrawal is that one minute I was afraid I might die, the next minute I was afraid I might not.

Accidents

The number one cause of emergency room visits and 21 percent of all injuries is alcohol (*Alcoholism: Clinical and Experimental Research*, 2007). This includes injuries *to* someone who was drinking—crashes, slips/falls—*by* someone who was drinking—injured in an OWI crash—or injured *by drinking*—gastritis or drug interactions. Two hospital admissions each minute are attributable to alcohol directly (*North West Public Health Observatory*, September 2010). This was a 9.5 percent increase of prior years and a 65 percent increase over five years.

... 30 percent of transportation injuries are alcohol-related
... 22 percent of the 12 million home-accident injuries in 2012 were alcohol-related
... 58 percent of fire fatalities have alcohol in their systems, which presumably kept them from fleeing safely
... 45 percent of drownings are alcohol-related
... 15.5 percent of occupational injuries are alcohol-related
... And 56 percent of assault *victims* have alcohol in their bodies ... when you drink you are at a two-and-a-half-times greater risk of a violent death.

A Norwegian study in 2011 co-authored by professor Thor Norstom (reported in *Addiction* magazine, November 2011) demonstrated that extending bar time by one hour led to an increase in violence of approximately 16 percent per year. The results suggest the effect occurs both ways, meaning closing bars one hour earlier led to a 16 percent decreases. Either way, it backs up what I saw covering the Dallas Knife and Gun Club at Parkland Hospital in Dallas, Texas, as a reporter on weekends.

The media has overemphasized alcohol's role in car wrecks but has under-reported the role of alcohol in other violent or accidental deaths. A 2012 Ohio State University study concluded that news organizations failure to report alcohol in those cases dampens public support of alcohol-control laws or abstinence.

Indirect health consequences

Alcohol itself is toxic. It's broken down in the body in the following sequence:

Alcohol>Acetaldehyde>Acetic Acid (vinegar)>Water+CO^2

The first metabolite, acetaldehyde, is 30 times more toxic than alcohol and is responsible for damage to tissues. It irritates your body's membranes, causing tearing in the eyes, light intolerance, red eyes, runny nose, aches and pains, chills, headaches and fever ... because acetaldehyde is a *poison*. It's an extremely flammable industrial chemical used in paints and solvents.

Acetaldehyde has an OSHA Material Safety Data Sheet for those who handle it at plants and labs requiring hefty protective gear because it is so flammable and a suspected carcinogen. "Gloves (impervious). Lab coat. Vapor respirator. Be sure to use an approved/certified respirator or equivalent. Wear appropriate respirator when ventilation is inadequate. Splash goggles ... Flammable liquid. Keep away from heat. Keep away from sources of ignition. Stop leak if without risk. Absorb with DRY earth, sand or other non-combustible material. Do not touch spilled material. Prevent entry into sewers, basements or confined areas ..." And we don't prevent entry into our bodies: We invite it into our bodies when we drink.

Pour it on grass, grass dies. Pour it in a river, it's hazmat. Pour it into the body as alcohol and it changes tissues, irritating them immediately and often changing them permanently.

Studies in Italy in 2010 with foundry workers discovered that tissues exposed to even low levels of toxic pollutants caused damage *at the DNA level* after only three days exposure. Three days. The relationship between chemicals and your DNA is part of a field called epigenetics and epigenetics is now showing that the alcohol you consume and its acetaldehyde byproduct leave a biological imprint on your DNA, one that can surface in diseases later (*Wall Street Journal*, February 28, 2012). If the drinking doesn't kill you immediately, it can kill you years down the road. Drinking often or in excess or both is like you've stepped out onto the highway: The truck just hasn't hit you yet.

The weight of scientific evidence demonstrates a link between alcohol and a greater risk of mortality for diseases of the immunological, nervous, cardiovascular, and respiratory and digestive systems. This was most recently confirmed by researcher Domenico Palli, a scientist at the Cancer Research and Prevention Institute of Florence in 2012, and new links with diseases and alcohol are being reported nearly weekly.

Absence of evidence is not evidence of absence. If you don't have the following conditions now, there are provable connections to getting them years after abstinence.

Heart disease

Heart disease is a leading cause of death in the U.S. and carries a definite link to alcohol despite French studies showing low amounts of red wine *benefiting* the circulatory system.

Acetaldehyde causes hypertension, a.k.a. high blood pressure. In a 2007 Medical University of South Carolina study, 120 alcohol users charted lower blood pressure only 12 weeks after abstaining.

Alcohol itself raids the body of vitamin B (Thiamin) which is essential for a healthy heart. B-deficiency enlarges the heart and creates distended neck veins, narrow pulse pressure, elevated diastolic blood pressure (the second number in your BP) and peripheral edema. Acetaldehyde also physically weakens muscle, the heart being your body's most important one. Think of how your tongue is weakened from drinking (slurring) and your legs are weakened (wobbliness) and the same thing is happening to your heart. However, with the heart, the weakening causes damage that accumulates.

Acetaldehyde also increases cholesterol, especially triglycerides. High cholesterol is a leading indicator of heart trouble on the horizon and the number one condition treated with prescription drugs in the U.S.

Brain damage/disease

Cadaever brains have provided conclusive evidence of a brain atrophying (shrinking) after alcohol misuse. However, Dr Ernest Noble of University of California—Irvine says, "Brain damage caused by alcohol, in relatively small quantities can affect the ability of brain cells to make proteins and RNA . . . essential for metabolism and organization of all cells as well as their ability to duplicate themselves." A former social drinker, he quit drinking at all upon conclusion of his study.

A 2012 study similarly indicates that moderate drinking reduces the production of new brain cells by 40 percent. The November 8, 2012 journal, *Neuorscience*, reports the level of alcohol intake was not enough to impair the motor skills of the rats in the study, however, the decrease in the brain's ability to create new cells could have profound effects on learning and memory later. The area of the brain that produces the neuron cells is the hippocampus, which is associated with learning and memory. Affecting this part of the brain might not be something you notice immediately, but over time, weekly drinking could have so dramatically reduced the neurons that learning or remembering things becomes more difficult. The study indicates that people don't have to be alcoholic to do damage to brain structures and that social drinking may be more harmful to people than is currently perceived by the general public.

The impact on mental health and the many fingers of the mind are varied. On one hand there are those who endure years of heavy drinking with the mind's fingers remaining as nimble as a pianist's. Others emerge not so deft. It is believed alcohol increases the chances for Alzheimer's and earlier onset of dementia. Stanford University research in 2010 also proved that alcohol use disorders cause deficits in working memory and visio-spatial abilities (think: coordination) even after abstinence.

Sociologist William Anixter pointed out in 1990 before the Anxiety Disorders Association's Washington, DC, conference that 80 percent of Alcoholics suffer from depression. The unanswered question more than two decades later is how much of that was there organically and how much was caused by the alcohol/acetaldehyde. A 2007 study does make the connection between Alcoholic liver disease and the mind. The frontal cortex—responsible for reasoning and memory—is more impaired in patients when they have cirrhosis.

Liver damage/disease

The alcohol user is eight times more likely to get cirrhosis, which is irreversible, incurable and fatal. There was a time when the *only* disease people, including doctors, linked to alcohol was cirrhosis. Not so anymore, but it is still almost exclusively a drinker's disease, only rarely caused by something other than alcohol (e.g. viruses or other infections).

Not all Alcoholics will get it. Only one in 10 develops cirrhosis. However, it is not the only liver disease cause by alcohol/acetaldehyde. A fatty liver occurs when alcohol consumption disrupts how the body chooses its fuel. Cell mitochondria—our body power plants—normally use fat to produce energy. As acetaldehyde breaks down in the body it releases hydrogen, which mitochondria use before fat as fuel. The unused fat then accumulates around the liver. Even in someone who doesn't look fat in their extremities or midsection, fat deposits choke the liver.

Alcoholic hepatitis is a third type of liver injury connected to alcohol misuse. It is a condition similar to the other hepatitis diseases, but is not the same as A, B or C hepatitis.

Lest you think these three liver problems are the realm of only the hard drinker, they can be stimulated by amounts of alcohol between seven and 13 ounces of whiskey—five to nine shots or mixed drinks—in 24 hours.

There are very few symptoms of liver injury until it becomes chronic because the liver has no pain nerves to tell you when it is hurt. If the liver had nerve endings, you'd never make it to the second drink.

Pancreatic damage

The pancreas is a long, flattened, pear-shaped organ located behind the stomach. It makes digestive enzymes and hormones including insulin. Alcohol users are 1.6 times more likely to develop pancreatic cancer, the most fatal of cancers. (Dr. Mirjam Heinen, Maastricht University, Netherlands, May 2009).

Men should be especially conscious of alcohol/acetaldehyde when it comes to the pancreas. University of Pittsburgh School of Medicine researchers isolated a gene variant in men that puts those who drink heavily at risk for pancreatitis. The researcher's report, released in November 2012 in the journal *Nature Genetics* found the genetic defect in half the men with alcoholic pancreatitis.

Pancreatitis is a disease in which the pancreas becomes inflamed. In pancreatitis, the digestive enzymes attack the tissue that produces them. Acute pancreatitis occurs suddenly, with severe upper abdominal pain and can be a serious, life-threatening illness if not treated. The most common symptoms of pancreatitis are acute abdominal pain, pain radiating into the back, nausea, vomiting and fever. The symptoms may last for a few days then disappear off and on.

Alcohol abuse and Alcoholism are risk factors for developing the disease, but the 2012 research shows men with a flaw on the X chromosome are more likely to have pancreatic troubles if they drink heavily. Women with the same flaw were not as likely to get the disease. The study suggests the second X chromosome in women protects them, while men have only one X chromosome and a Y. The gene doesn't cause pancreatitis but increases the risk in drinkers.

"The discovery that chronic pancreatitis has a genetic basis solves a major mystery about why some people develop chronic pancreatitis and others do not," study lead author Dr. David Whitcomb, professor of medicine, cell biology and physiology, and human genetics, said in a university news release. "We always knew there was an unexpected higher risk of men developing pancreatitis with alcohol consumption, but until now we weren't sure why," he said. "Our discovery of this new genetic variant on chromosome X helps explain this mystery as well."

Muscle disease

Acetaldehyde fragments muscle fibers, weakening them and allowing them to tear easily. Muscle atrophy or destruction can occur fairly easily. The weakness and atrophy have been known to medicine for 200 years as myopathy, but myopathy has come to be known as a common side effect of acetaldehyde and could provide a definitive lab test to separate Alcoholism from alcohol abuse. Sub-clinical myopathy has no symptoms but is identified by higher blood levels of a chemical known as CPK (creatine phosphokinase, for those looking for more geekspeak). An Alcoholic will have elevated CPK, an alcohol abuser won't. Taken in combination with elevated triglycerides on a liver blood test, it is a sure distinction between a person with the disease and someone who's simply an alcohol abuser. *The two tests together are the canary in the coal mine.* These blood tests can be more helpful in determining a course of treatment than the standardized fill-in-the-blank tests people can easily fool. (See pages 37-40 of *What the Early Worm Gets.*)

Breast cancer

One out of eight women will have an encounter with breast cancer. Alcohol use is the ONLY dietary factor increasing the likelihood of getting breast cancer.

Breast cancer risks increase 10 percent for every 10 grams of alcohol consumed daily. That's about *one drink*. (*Journal of the American Medical Association*, November 2, 2011) Women who consumed even "modest" alcohol (equivalent to 3-6 glasses of wine per week) were linked with a 15 percent increase of developing the disease. Researchers also found that the increased risk of breast cancer for those who drank at least 30 grams of alcohol per day on average (at least two drinks daily) was 51 percent higher compared to women who never drank alcohol.

In addition, when the researchers looked at alcohol consumption levels between the ages 18 to 40 and after the age of 40, they discovered that both were strongly linked with an increased risk of breast cancer. The connection with alcohol consumption still remained even after controlling, reducing or quitting alcohol consumption after the age of 40.

Stomach disease

Gastritis—sharp stomach pains—and gastric ulcers are very common results of regular alcohol use and can last for years after abstinence. Alcohol slows the emptying of the stomach, which allows more acid to build up in the stomach and therefore more time for it to permanently damage the stomach lining. Cancer of the stomach is called gastric cancer. Gastric adenocarcinoma is the most common type of stomach cancer. It arises from those cells in the stomach lining.

Chronic gastritis also is a predisposing factor in developing stomach cancer ("Alcohol and stomach cancer in northern Italy," in the *Nutrition Research Newsletter*, September 1994) The newsletter concluded, "heavy intake of total alcohol (at least eight drinks/day) or wine (six to eight or at least eight drinks/day) was associated with a small but significant increase in stomach cancer risk."

A more recent study put the cancer risk in much more exact and troubling terms. Researchers evaluated information from the European Prospective Investigation into Cancer and Nutrition (EPIC) study. ("Alcohol consumption and gastric cancer risk in the European Prospective Investigation into Cancer and Nutrition (EPIC) cohort," in the *American Journal of Clinical Nutrition*, October 2011) More than 400 cases of stomach cancer were diagnosed among study participants. Heavy alcohol consumption increased the risk of stomach cancer in men. Men who consumed an average of more than four drinks per day were 65 percent more likely to develop stomach cancer than men who were very light drinkers. The link between alcohol and stomach cancer appeared to be stronger for beer than for wine or spirits.

Other cancers

Dr. Palli's 2012 research identified "significantly" higher risks for cancers of the pharynx, oral cavity and larynx and higher rates for cancers of the esophagus and rectum. "Alcohol's role as a dietary carcinogen emerged quite clearly," said Palli. (*Alcoholism: Clinical and Experimental Research*, February 2012) An older study put the numbers at an estimated 75 percent of esophageal cancers in the U.S. are attributable to chronic, excessive alcohol consumption and nearly 50 percent of cancers of the mouth, pharynx, and larynx are associated with heavy drinking. (F.S. Stinson and S.F. DeBakey, "Alcohol-related mortality in the United States, 1979-1988," in the *British Journal of Addiction*, 1992)

According to Annual Review of Pharmacology and Toxicology in 1990, alcohol misuse results in abnormalities in the way the body processes nutrients and may subsequently promote certain types of cancer later in life. Malnutrition is so common during our drinking careers because our calories are empty ones. There are about 1300 calories in a pint of vodka . . . no protein, minerals, vitamins or fiber. Acetaldehyde raids the body's B vitamins and breaks down amino acid chains rendering them dietarily useless. Iron levels are remarkably low in practicing Alcoholics. Living like this, with reduced levels of iron, zinc, vitamin E and some of the B vitamins, has been experimentally associated with several cancers. Alcoholism also has been associated with suppression of the immune system. Immune suppression makes you more susceptible to various infectious diseases and, theoretically, to cancer. (G. Roselle, "Alcohol and the immune system," in *Alcohol Health & Research World*, 1992)

Nerve disease/neuropathy

Alcoholic neuropathy is identical to the neuropathy experienced as a side effect of diabetes. Neuropathy causes a tingling of burning sensation, or a loss of sensation all together. In Alcoholics, as with diabetics, it is an affliction of the limbs and especially the legs. Commonly there is a reduced sensitivity in the feet. You're not able to feel pain. When this happens, foot injuries, like blisters, can become infected so severely because you cannot feel pain that amputation is necessary. But the fatal problem with the neuropathy is the increase in the risk of stroke it carries.

Those two or three beers . . . not so benign now, are they?

If C2H3OH (alcohol) was a new food additive, over-the-counter remedy or dietary supplement before the FDA today for approval, with these documented side effects—*any single one of them*—it would be rejected. Transfat was chased out of our food system for less, ephedra banned for less.

However, most of these disease links with alcohol are not new, only bolstered by new and better research. You haven't noticed the slow trickling out of these studies individually but you do sit up when all of the things to which alcohol contributes are laid out one after another as they are in the last few pages. It's as offensive as the Mac story.

We've known many of these connections since the first Special Report to the U.S. Congress on Alcohol & Health in December, 1971. The National Institute on Alcohol Abuse and Alcoholism was created by the 1970 Hughes Act to develop and conduct comprehensive health, education, training, research and planning programs for the prevention and treatment of alcohol use disorders. They're tracking these nasty stats. And powerful special interests counter each one with commercials and bikini-clad bargirls.

You cannot take the relaxation value of alcohol without the side effects.

I worked for a couple of large insurers. Do you know why they probe about your drinking history? Because people die from alcohol. It shortens life expectancy by 10-12 years. People who don't die sooner have more sickness, even long after abstaining. Rates go up.

That 10-12 years is the conservative estimate by the way: A study conducted by the Centers for Disease Control and Prevention in 2005 found that alcohol misuse shortens the lives of this group by at least 30 years.

There is a logical, obvious conclusion of what this chemical does to the healthcare system and new governmental healthcare schemes. Even life-long abstainers pay for alcohol's damage because they're all paying premiums and taxes that cover health costs. If you want to reduce costs, reduce what is driving them. And that, in part, means making sure Alcoholics have resources to prevent lapse once they are sober. Every U.S. citizen is a stakeholder now under Obamacare in the success or failure of how alcohol use disorders are handled and how the Symptoms of Sobriety are managed.

We can't hope for better access to healthcare, cheaper premiums and lower taxes if we do not help people from drinking themselves into the system. We are turning more non-drinkers into Alcoholics presently than we are turning Alcoholics into non-drinkers. As a community, we're stigmatizing those who want to get out and stay out of the system and at the same time are glamorizing the drinkers who haven't had trouble. Yet.

Drinking isn't illegal. Successive approximation—a psychologist's term for the notion that success is more fun but failure is a better teacher—suggests alcohol should stay legal given how poorly Prohibition went. We don't even drink today as much as our nation's settlers did, so we've progressed since pioneer days and Prohibition. But as a point of fact: They didn't know the facts back then; Today we *act* as if we don't. The status quo—$221 billion a year—is not sustainable. Or acceptable.

We presently spend more in America on pills for erectile dysfunction than on the education, prevention and treatment for our number one killer. Our best thinking as a country got us here. When the National Institutes of Health estimates $1.93 in healthcare savings and increased productivity for every $1 spent on alcohol education, research and treatment, thinking with our boners might not be our best way forward. Nearly nine percent of U.S. workers are drinking in ways that contribute to absenteeism, higher health costs and lost productivity. To my knowledge, erection problems do not have the same adverse economic impact.

In 2008, Congress passed a $15 billion AIDS initiative. Fifteen billion. That's the largest global health initiative ever to combat a specific disease . . . in Africa. One baby born with AIDS every 45 seconds half a planet away was a bigger health concern for Congress than two Americans hospitalized each minute because of alcohol. We have an American epidemic by any measure of epidemiology, but we seem content to allow it to be the elephant in the room.

In recent years we've emphasized other things in our public descriptions of "epidemics." We've focused on smoke-free living or obesity-control programs in public health to address these epidemics. Alcohol use disorders are bigger than those two epidemics combined.

The lion's share of medical research goes to cancer in the U.S. However, the accurate assessment and treatment, not mistreatment, of Alcoholism will be the next great frontier in medicine because of how alcohol interconnects with so many other diseases, cancers and social problems. More and more scientific discoveries *are* taking place. We're on the brink of breakthroughs in the puzzling area of biochemistry and cortisol. The field of alcohology is wide open for exploration and application. Part of application is how we better manage the Symptoms of Sobriety to keep former drinkers, former drinkers. My personal experience is one of thousands every year where the best research and knowledge of what works in treatment isn't even applied. Fortunately, I made it through that application problem and bridged a gulf between a weak program with Mac and a place to communicate through my Symptoms. It's safer for all if we do a better job of applying all these stellar breakthroughs because not only did I nearly take my own life, but I could easily have taken down someone with me when I drank and drove.

While the system is in need of repair, each of us is in repair, too. The stressors are the dark times, the Symptoms of Sobriety are the clouds. They aren't good feelings or emotions on which to dwell but they'll create a storm if ignored. Knowing the stressors and handling them appropriately can help you turn toward the good feelings to cherish, the silver linings to enjoy. As I started the book I pointed out that sobriety was what I thought would be the silver lining to the disease, only to discover that it had its own clouds. As I end the book, I'm enthusiastic about the good stuff that happens when you don't drink in response to the Symptoms. Not every day has clouds. I'm no meteorologist and can't predict when they'll return, but at least I know I'll go talk to someone to make them manageable.

> *"Never consider yourself a weak or fallen creature. Whatever may have happened up to now may be because you didn't know. But now, be careful."*—Swami Brahmananda Saraswati

Appendix I

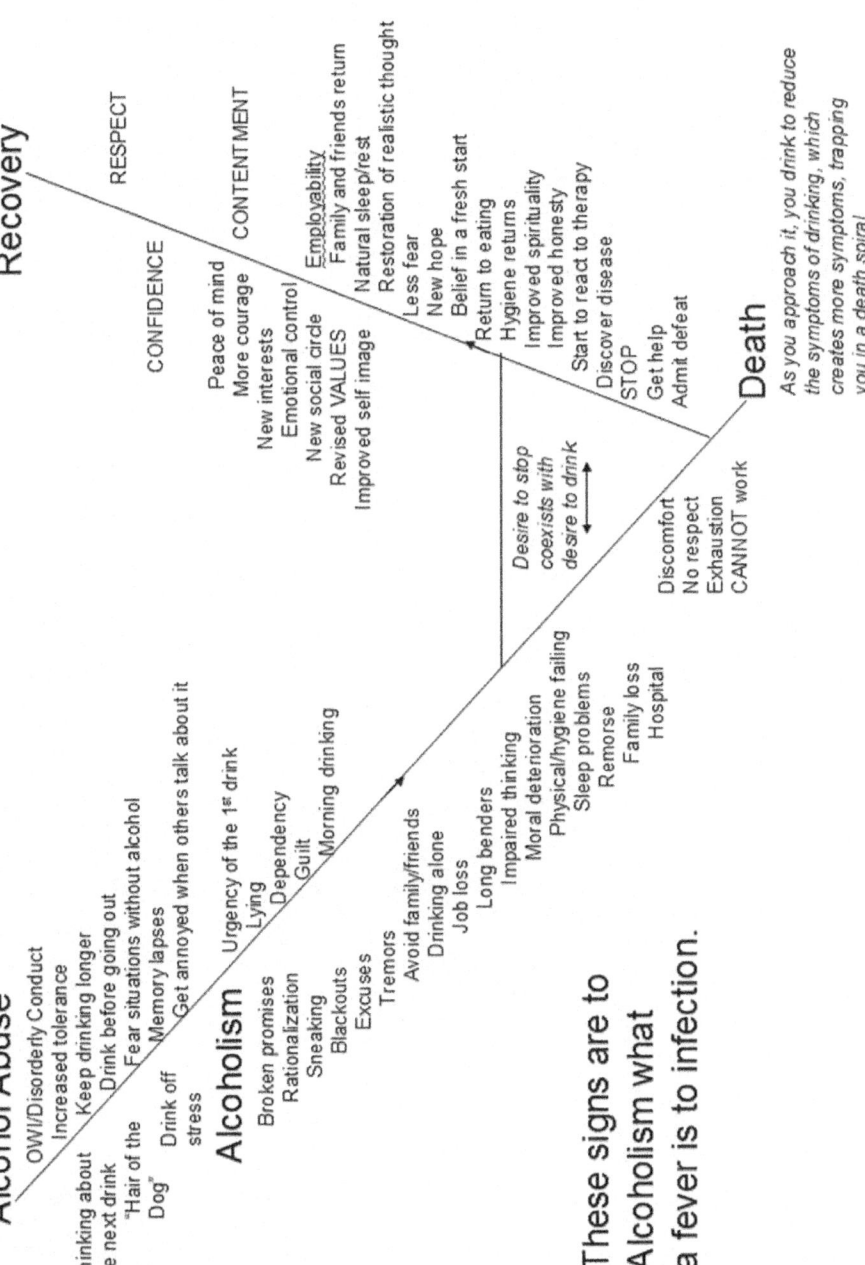

Appendix II

Alcoholism vs. Alcohol Abuse

	Alcoholism ("Drinking Problem")	AlcoholAbuse ("Problem Drinker")
Directly Affects	8% of population	16-25% of population
Clinical View	Disease *Chronic, Primary, Progressive, Fatal*	Not a disease
Diagnostic Definition	Three or more of the following: 1. Increased tolerance *Need more to achieve result/effects diminish with use of the same amt.* 2. Withdrawal or alcoholic consumption to avoid it 3. Alcohol use for prolonged periods or increased amounts 4. Persistent desire 5. Unsuccessful effort to control/reduce or quit 6. Considerable time dedicated to use 7. Avoidance of social/work/recreational activity in favor of use 8. Alcohol use continues despite phys. problems	One or more of the following: 1. Failure to fulfill roles as a result of drinking 2. Recurrent drinking in physically dangerous situations 3. Recurrent legal difficulties 4. Continued consumption despite #3
Craving	Craves every drink AFTER the first. He is at ease with alcohol, dreading the first one but has more cravings after 10 drinks than before the first, long after everyone else stops	Craves the FIRST drink. He's at ease with alcohol. He can have enough after several.
Foundation	Biological *Genetic, neurochemically based*	Mental *Behaviorally based*
Aggravated by	Stress, emotion	Social environment
Prognosis	Permanent and progresses even while abstinent but can be halted with appropriate treatment	100% curable
Amount and frequency	Not controllable *Abstinence is only realistic outcome vs. death*	Controllable *moderation is a possible outcome*
Telling characteristic	Wants to stop but can't	Can stop but won't

Made in the USA
Coppell, TX
21 November 2023